MYLES MUNROE

REDISCOVERING THE
KINGDOM

*ANCIENT HOPE
FOR OUR
21ST CENTURY WORLD*

Destiny Image® Publishers, Inc.

P.O. Box 310
Shippensburg, PA 17257-0310

"Speaking to the Purposes of God for This Generation
and for the Generations to Come"

Bahamas Faith Ministry

P.O. Box N9583
Nassau, Bahamas

Hardcover ISBN 0-7684-2217-5
Paperback ISBN 0-7684-2257-4

For Worldwide Distribution
Printed in the U.S.A.

This book and all other Destiny Image, Revival Press, MercyPlace,
Fresh Bread, Destiny Image Fiction, and Treasure House books are available
at Christian bookstores and distributors worldwide.

Hardcover: 7 8 9 10 11 / 09 08 07 06 05
Paperback: 3 4 5 6 7 8 9 10 11 / 09 08 07 06 05

For a U.S. bookstore nearest you, call
1-800-722-6774.

For more information on foreign distributors, call
717-532-3040.

Or reach us on the Internet:
www.destinyimage.com

DEDICATION

*T*o the millions of religious people around the world working tirelessly to fulfill the hunger that still exists after all the rituals, customs, traditions, formalities, and work—may this book bring comfort to your mourning soul.

To the late Alma Trottman—your life and legacy live on in our memories and thoughts of you. You truly lived a Kingdom-filled life and I know your time with the King now is like Esther. Perhaps you are both together enjoying royalty at its best.

To the youth of our world—may your generation never have to struggle through religion to find the joy of the Kingdom.

To the King eternal, immortal, the all wise God, and my Lord, Jesus Christ—may Your Kingdom and Your will be done on earth just as it is in heaven.

TABLE OF CONTENTS

ACKNOWLEDGMENTS

This book has taken more than 20 years to prepare and three years to write, and many people encouraged me during the entire process. There were times when it seemed like I would never get through it. However, with persistence and a keen focus, it is finally complete. I want to acknowledge everyone who participated for their help and support, without which this project would never have been finished.

Nothing in life is ever successful without the corporate effort of many gifted people who were willing to network and submit their talent, experience, and passion for a common goal. I am always reminded that we are the sum total of all the people we have known, met, and learned from. This work is the product of countless individuals whose thoughts, ideas, perspectives, and work have given me the exposure to the knowledge I have placed in this book.

I wish to thank my wife, Ruth, and our children, Charisa and Chairo (Myles Jr.), for their patience and understanding during my endless travels and late-night writing. My achievements are yours, also.

To Don Milam, my excellent editorial advisor and guide in developing this manuscript—you are an author's dream and a gift to many who will read this work. Thank you for pursuing me to get this done.

To all the members and staff of our ministry in Nassau, Bahamas, and around the world—thank you for allowing me to develop and refine these ideas and concepts by sharing and testing them with you. May His Kingdom come through you!

PREFACE

The greatest threat to the future of the world is religion. Nuclear weapons, terrorism, SARS, shifting governments, military coups, and AIDS are simply tools used by religion. More wars have been fought in the name of religion than any other influence. Millions have died over the past 2,000 years under the destructive hand of religious zeal. Misplaced and misguided religious passion has produced such historical scars as the Crusades, the Inquisition, ethnic cleansing, and the horror of the Holocaust.

Why is religion so powerful and controlling? Why is it more powerful than politics, military arms, and scientific advancement? Because religion is not just a social, cultural, political, or ideological factor; instead it finds its power in the personal chambers of the soul of the individual. Within the soul we discover the source of the private motivation that forms perceptions and behavior. Man is more willing to die for the sake of his religion than for any political, social, or ideological reason.

Religion is as old as mankind, finding its roots in the private recesses of the human spirit. Every culture, no matter how old or far removed, has developed some form of religious practice that attempts to satisfy an elusive vacuum in the pit of the human soul crying out for reason, purpose, and significance. For mankind, life on planet earth has been nothing more than a long tedious march down the road of time, with each new generation searching for something they cannot define. The long chains of civilizations have left undeniable imprints on the pages of history—evidences for our generation that the search continues. From the secrets etched on the walls of ancient caves to the grand archaeological monuments to the remnants of the great empires, man marches on seeking to find himself and make sense of his world. Man's travels through this world have produced a tapestry of religious practices and ideologies that only serve to create more problems than they solve.

A brief look at our modern, sophisticated, technocratic, cyberspace-age world of today can be the source of fear, depression, discouragement, insecurity, and uncertainty. From the archaic world of the cave men and bush hunters through the progressive succession of agrarian cultures, to the advent of the industrial revolution leading to the scientific age of post-modernism and the computer age, we are still no better than nor different from our ancestors of old.

The only difference seems to be the sophistication of our tools and weapons. We are smarter but not wiser; we live longer but not healthier; we have more but enjoy less; we can go to the moon, but we cannot go home to a good family; we have access to more information but know less about life. Tragically, we protect whales, but kill our children; we improve the quality of our food but produce less healthy strains for our consumption; we have more religion but less love; and we blame others for our choices as we look to ourselves for solutions to the problems we create.

The 21st century seems to be more uncertain than all the previous centuries in history. Planet earth is spinning through the solar system like a spaceship without a compass as it travels on a course to self-destruction. On this long march of humanity, mankind has invented and developed a variety of systems and social structures in its attempt to grapple with the realities of life on our global spaceship. Over the centuries we have watched the creation of a variety of governmental systems including demigods, dictatorships, monarchies, and tyrannies, as well as the theories and practices of socialism, democracy, communism, and imperialism. Each of them has had an opportunity to try to make life better and more "humane" on our great planet. However, wars have increased rather than decreased, weapons of mass destruction are more available than ever before, and fear for safety and security is greater than ever before in history. All governments—even the best form we have developed, democracy—have failed to realize the world we keep searching for.

Two of the greatest tragedies of our modern history were World War I and World War II, when millions lost their lives at the hands of their fellow planet-dwellers. After World War I, various leaders joined together and made a promise that it would never happen again. They created the League of Nations, an organization dedicated to promoting world peace and initiating reasonable solutions to human conflicts. However, this pipe dream ended in the explosion of World War II.

After that conflict ended, world leaders made a second commitment, determining once again to never allow mankind to spiral down into the death-dealing clutches of international war. This commitment gave birth to the United Nations, a world body dedicated to making and keeping the peace around the world. Yet, more wars have been fought since the formation of the United Nations than before its creation. Today, as wars continue to ravage our planet, the United Nations itself, along with its purpose and usefulness, is under serious scrutiny.

I find it ironic that most of the current wars and tensions are products of, or strongly influenced by, religions. Where do we go from here? What do we do? What is the answer? Why can't we just live together? Why is mankind so frustrated? Why do our cultures keep clashing into each other and why are our children on the streets killing one another?

These are the questions that this book is attempting to answer. The solution to our dilemma is somewhere in the middle of our search. It makes sense to conclude that if our world has no answers to the questions it asks and no solutions to the problems it creates, then it might be wise to look to another world for help. *Rediscovering the Kingdom* answers this very proposition. I am not talking about some weird, impractical, illusive, metaphysical notion of a pie in the sky, but rather a reasonable, tangible, human-friendly solution that responds not only to our unspoken desires about life here on earth but beyond.

This book is about you and your passion to understand life. It is about your search for control over your circumstances and destiny. It is about living life to its fullest and about reconnecting to your true self. You were created not just to exist but to live a fulfilled and significant life. This book is about that life—your life! Join me as we seek to discover an alternative reality at the end of man's long search for truth.

HIDDEN TREASURE

T he old lady was dressed in what seemed like seven dresses. Her fingers were exposed despite the fact that she wore a pair of life-worn gloves. She pushed an old shopping cart that testified that it was her mobile home, and she lived at the mercy of the elements. Her face showed the wear and tear of years of living. She was bent over, looking in a garbage can, searching for life-sustaining remains discarded by the more fortunate of society.

Suddenly, she shot up out of the barrel and shouted, "I found it. I found it!" There between her thumb and index finger she held the most beautiful pearl.

I ran over to her and asked if I could help her. She smiled and shook her head with a confidence I did not expect from one in her status of life. Then she proceeded to tell me the story of her life that still impacts me today.

She told of how she was born into a wealthy family and that her grandfather had left a treasure for her before she was born. During her infant years a fire had destroyed her family home, which was once on the site where the barrel of garbage now stood. The result was that her family lost everything, including the chest that held the treasure from her grandfather. She came to that spot every day to search for that treasure. Many people who knew her story would give her handouts to wear and leftovers to eat. But she said she believed that if she ever found that one treasure, then she would have all of her needs met and be able to repurchase the property lost by her family and rebuild the family house that was destroyed.

Today was her lucky day—she found the treasure. For many years she had only heard about it and had descriptions of it, but now she actually had it. Her life was changed that day, and her search was over. She regained her status and position in life and gave up all her life's struggles for the sake of that one treasure.

It was a pearl. May you find your own pearl in these pages.

MATTHEW 13:44-47

The kingdom of heaven is like treasure hidden in a field. When a man found it, he hid it again, and then in his joy went and sold all he had and bought that field.

Again, the kingdom of heaven is like a merchant looking for fine pearls. When he found one of great value, he went away and sold everything he had and bought it.

"An idea is more powerful than an army."

INTRODUCTION

There is nothing more powerful than an idea. Ideas created and now control the world we live in. When an idea is conceived it is called a thought; when a thought is conceived it is called a concept. Concepts are the material that dreams are made of and they serve as the substance for living and interpreting life. Everything humans have made or invented was first preceded by an idea. As a matter of fact, inventions are often called one's "brain-child." In essence, the mind can be impregnated by ideas that develop into concepts that become visions that produce reality.

Concepts are to life what the blood is to the body. Perhaps this is what the great king Solomon meant when he wrote over 3,000 years ago, *"As a man thinks so is he."* You are and become your concepts. Psychologists describe our value and estimation of our life by the nature of our "self-concept."

Concepts rise in value as we consider our perception and interpretation of life. Human communication is solely dependent on concepts. We can only understand life to the degree that our concepts are correct. As a matter of fact, the purpose and goal of communication is to transfer your ideas and concepts from *your* mind to *another* mind. Therefore, communication is only successful when the sender's concepts are received accurately and properly understood by the receiver and vice versa.

If your ideas are wrong then your concepts are wrong, and consequently, your understanding will be inaccurate and incomplete. You can only understand properly if your concepts are in alignment with your ideas and your ideas must be based upon God's dynamic truth. The original concept is always in the mind of the sender. In this state of the thinking process it is called a "precept." Simply put, a *precept* is "an original idea." Therefore, in order to understand the original concept, you must have a clear grasp of the precepts of the sender of a message. The heart of understanding is precepts and concepts. Error is a product and a result of what is called "mis-conception." In reality, the receiver misunderstood the concept of the sender.

This book will fail in its purpose and intent if I do not successfully convey and transfer my precepts, concepts, ideas, and thoughts to you the reader. So let's proceed in exploring the critical concepts that lead to the answer to man's search for meaning.

THE LONG SEARCH FOR THE IDEAL

In every generation, since the beginning of time, the dream of a utopian society has motivated and sustained the passion of mankind, producing highly developed cultures and social systems as they moved forward in this pursuit. The driving force and desire for the perfect world finds its way into every civilization and has been the source of inspiration that has led to the invention of philosophical ideas, social infrastructures, and even religions, all having some kind of impact on our contemporary communities. This force is centralized in man's search for the ideal.

Passion for the ideal produced in many ancient cultures the dream of a messianic vision. This is the belief that somewhere in some distant future from some unknown place a person would come who would provide the answers to all our problems. He would establish the "ideal world" free from pain, hatred, fear, poverty, and other social ills—a world of peace, love, joy, and harmony among all mankind.

This search and desire for an idyllic world is the source of the development of the concept called "ideology." Ideology is the most powerful energy that has impacted the lives of people over thousands of years and continues its effects to this very day. An ideology is the formulation of ideas and thoughts that have been pondered, developed, refined, defined, and formalized. These ideas are also defined as a philosophy, or "a way of thinking." Some of these "formalized ideas" have produced "schools of thought," which became the foundations of theoretical and ideological premises for the creation of systems of governing communities, societies, cities, nations, and the world. On the negative side, some of these ideologies have been the source of injustice, destruction, oppression, mass poverty, depression, and social terror.

These ideologies have carried a variety of labels, and over thousands of years they have emerged, submerged, and then reemerged in succeeding generations. Some of these labels are quite familiar even in our generation: imperialism, socialism, communism, dictatorship, humanism, deism, democracy, monarchy, and communal living. Many of these have been tried, revised, integrated, revived, and have been the source of many social experiments.

Yet, no matter how much man has tried to re-create his world, the fulfillment of his hope and desire for "utopia" still eludes him. Our most recent attempts have led to the advent of the ideology of "individual freedom" and the admirable concept of "self-determination" and "a just society," which we have termed in our modern civilization as "the democratic ideal." Despite the fact that this is the most civil form of national governance and social relations within a society, even this has not manifested the utopia its founders dreamed of.

The motivation and inspiration for the pursuit of the civil society and the democratic ideal is the concept of "freedom." The pursuit of personal freedom is the strongest motivator in Western social consciousness. This desire to be free to pursue one's personal dreams and to maximize one's potential is the foundation of the democratic ideal and is embraced as the ultimate standard of a free society. However, the societies and communities that have tried this noble "freedom" experiment are still plagued with the inconsistencies of inequality, racism, prejudice, injustice, corruption, jealousy, suspicion, competition, abuse, neglect, and a clear disparity between the "haves" and "have-nots." In the end, mankind has become imprisoned by his pursuit of freedom.

THE SOURCE OF THE DESIRE

I have had the privilege of traveling to 70 nations and have worked with every race, culture, socio-economic class, and religious and political group, and yet I am still amazed that in each one of these societies the search is the same. In fact, it is my conclusion that we are all the same and searching for the same thing. What makes us different is the route and systems we implement and develop to find what we are searching for. Simply put, all people are the same and looking for the same answers to the same questions.

A few years ago I received a gift from some friends in a faraway country with whom I had the opportunity to work. Their culture and social background was different from my own. They had heard me speak on the subject of man's search for meaning and purpose in life. The gift they gave me was a beautiful hardbound book with a title that still sticks in my mind 20 years later. The book was called *The Long Search*. I was intrigued with this simple title but, even more than that, I was pleasantly surprised by the content of the book. It has become one of my favorite books in my personal library.

The book chronicled the history of the invention, development, refinement, and practices of all religions in the world. The photos captured my imagination, the text expanded my appreciation of the complex nature of religions, and the research provided insight into the commonality of the human family. At the heart of the book was the concept that all religions are a result of man's search for a Supreme Being—identified as "God," "divinity," or whatever other word one chooses to fill in the blank. Religion is man's attempt to respond to his desire to find some type of meaningful, and possibly intimate, relationship with a Supreme Being as he seeks to find some reasonable meaning to life.

This human search for Ultimate Reality is natural and common to all human cultures—even the self-acclaimed atheist inherently believes that, at the very least, there is someone or something out there not to believe in. Even in the most primitive societies we find this expression of desire to seek, find, and understand a Supreme Being as evidenced in the creation, development, and practice of some form of religion.

However, the question confronts us: from where did this natural desire and need to seek for a higher power originate? This internal soul-searching irritation—that there must be a reason and design for the universe and creation—must have a source. The "long search" for reality obviously implies that something is lost. It is impossible to search for nothing. Therefore it is my contention that the very nature of man's soul search indicates that something he previously possessed is missing.

It also seems that this need to search is not a *choice* but a *necessity*. The search is personal as well as corporate. Perhaps the best way to find what is missing and what we are searching for is to identify what you need or desire. For example, thirst implies the need for water, hunger implies the need for food, and tiredness implies the need for rest.

So, we can identify what we lack by what we naturally desire and thus recognize our need. We will discuss this need of mankind in succeeding chapters. However it is important to at least acknowledge its existence and overpowering control over all mankind and to also appreciate that this deep need controls and dictates man's behavior, both individually and corporately.

Identifying the Need

I have spent over 40 years studying and researching this phenomenon, first in a personal pursuit and then also in a lifelong commitment to help others find some answers to their dilemma. I have come to the conclusion that the common pursuit of all humans is the pursuit of power, the desire to possess the ability to control one's circumstances and destiny. I know this may shock you and perhaps cause you to go into denial. Most of us would not want to admit that we desire something as frightening as power, but the reality is that this is the basic desire in every human heart.

When I use the term *power,* I am not referring to the tyrannical, oppressive, dictatorial control of people, but rather the ability to control one's own circumstances and environment. It is this lack of control over our daily lives, situations, and circumstances that makes us feel so helpless and live as victims of life. For most of us life is simply a daily struggle as we try to stay afloat in a sea of uncertainty and pressures of all sorts. At the same time we wrestle with a sense of *dignified* slavery to the institutions of our societies.

Our desire and passion to gain this power to control our circumstances and environment is the motivation for our behavior. We strive to gain positions of influence in order to accumulate financial wealth. We seek the power that money promises us: political and spiritual power, the accumulation of status symbols, superior knowledge, and many other forms of controlling dispositions. I believe this pursuit for power is simply the pursuit of dominion over life.

This human preoccupation and desire for power and dominion is also the fuel for man's obsession with progressive development in all disciplines including political science, social science, biological science, technical science, spiritual research, economic research, and all other aspects of the human experience. The result of this power search is found in the long human march toward modernization. Over the past 6,000 years mankind *has* tried and *continues* to try to control and tame the environment through the inventions of primitive and modern instruments. For example, in science he tries to stop the aging process, improve the quality and length of life, and produce every type of pill to solve a myriad of problems. Ultimately his greatest challenge is to prevent the reality of death.

Yet no matter how far man thinks he has progressed, the ability to achieve dominion and power over life and death on earth still eludes him. In fact, in light of all the uncontrollable social ills, health epidemics, military conflicts, political unrest, economic uncertainties, religious clashes, and destruction of the environment, it seems as if man's advancement is an evolution, backward in time.

This human failure to achieve control and mastery over his environment and circumstances has left him with a deep desire for a brand new world. The human spirit longs for a world he can control where circumstances are at the mercy of his will. This is the greatest human desire. This is also the source and motivation of religious and spiritual development and practice. In every religion we discover the component that promises power to control circumstances and even death itself. This explains why the deep dark secret practices of witchcraft and spiritism are so attractive to millions; they promise power over people and circumstances.

The human spirit is possessed by this desire to dominate, rule, and control the personal private world and the environment. Man is in search of the ultimate governing power of dominion. The desire for power is inherent in the human spirit. To understand this desire for power, it is necessary to understand the original purpose and design of mankind and the assignment for which he was created.

"There is no greater pursuit of man than the pursuit for power to control our circumstances."

DISCOVERING THE ORIGIN AND PURPOSE OF MAN

It was five o'clock in the morning and I had not slept all night. I was nervous and anxious. It was the big day—time for the test I dreaded. It was a memorable day during my years at the university. I had studied all night and faithfully read all my notes, books, and reviews. It was my final biology test. The focus of this class was the human anatomy.

At the end of the test I felt confident that I had done well. Three days later I was proven right when my professor called me in to congratulate me for receiving the top grade in the class. I was so proud of myself and felt I had achieved something outstanding. As I stood there looking at the papers he handed to me, I suddenly realized something I had never thought of. Throughout this course of study I had become well educated in the knowledge of the human body—the names, purposes, and functions all of its intricate parts and organs. The thought that struck me was that I knew what the human body was but did not know why the human *was*. In other words, I knew the *product* but did not know its *purpose*.

This youthful discovery still motivates me today. There are over 6 billion people on planet earth and only a few of them know why they exist. What a tragedy! Who is man? Why was man created? Why was he put on this planet? What is he to do? Where did he come from? What can he do? Where is he going? These questions strike at the heart of all human pursuit. All that men want to know are the answers to these questions.

Are humans simply a link in some evolutionary chain, as proclaimed by the theologians of evolution? Are we simply sophisticated primates participating in the drama of the survival of the fittest? Are we simply a freak accident of some cosmic big-bang mishap from which we emerged from the slime of some cosmic soup as the magnificent reasoning self-conscious being to which we have evolved today? I find it impossible to believe that anyone could believe such a theory. This unreasonable, unsubstantiated, unproven theoretical proposition has no foundation in truth and desecrates the truth of man's origin. It dilutes and diminishes his glorious purpose.

Man is the crowning act of an intentional Creator. He exists as God's co-regent in a world created for him. In examining mankind we will discover the beauty and the mystery of God's purpose for the whole of creation.

It seems that the end of all things will be discovered in the beginning of all things. Therefore, we will begin our study by considering God's original plan for His creation. Quite obviously, if we seek to understand the creation, we must first understand the Creator, because the original purpose of any product is only in the mind of the creator of that product. Therefore, to discover the purpose and reason for mankind's creation and existence, we must attempt to tap into the mind of his Creator. After all no one knows the product like the manufacturer.

THE ORIGIN OF THE FIRST KINGDOM

First, it is essential to understand that before anything was, God is. The word *God* denotes "self-existing one or self-sufficient one" and describes a being that needed nothing or no one to exist. Therefore "God" is not a name but rather a description of a character. Because of who and what He is, He alone qualifies for the title of God. This totally independent God existed before all things and began His creative process by first producing the entire invisible world, which we also have come to know as the "supera" or "above" natural world. This act of creation initiated the concept of "ruler" and "ruler-ship" as the Creator became the governor over a created realm. Another word for ruler is "king." God called this invisible realm or domain "heaven" and thus He became the King over the domain, heaven.

This was the beginning and creation of the first kingdom called "the invisible Kingdom of God." This was also the introduction of the

24

concept of "kingdom." This concept of "kingdom" is critical, essential, necessary, required, and imperative in order to understand, appreciate, and comprehend the purpose, intent, goal, and objectives of God and mankind's relationship to Him and the creation.

DIVINE MOTIVATION FOR CREATION

It is not unreasonable to ask why God, the King of heaven, would want to create sons in His image and a visible universe. Was He not satisfied and pleased with an invisible realm of angels and powers to rule? I believe the answer to these questions lies in understanding the very nature of God Himself. There is much about this great awesome, self-sustaining One that we do not, cannot, and may never know, but He has revealed enough of Himself to mankind to allow us to glimpse some of the magnificence of His nature and character.

One such characteristic is that "God is love" (1 John 4:8,16). Please note that He does not say that He "has" love but that He "is" love. This is an important distinction when it comes to understanding His motivation, because if God is love, then His actions would naturally or supernaturally be the manifestation of the nature of love. One of the obvious qualities of love is that love has to give and share itself. If this be so, then the very nature of God would be to desire to share His rulership and government. In essence, love is fulfilled when it gives and shares itself.

It is this inherent nature of love that motivated the King of heaven to create spirit children (called mankind) to share His Kingdom rulership. In other words, man was created for the purpose of rulership and leadership. This is why in the message of Jesus, when He described the age of the Kingdom of God and its provision for man, His indication was that this Kingdom belonged to man before earth was created.

Then the King will say to those on His right, "Come, you who are blessed by My Father; take your inheritance, the kingdom prepared for you since the creation of the world" (Matthew 25:34).

It was God's idea to share His invisible Kingdom with His offspring, which He called mankind, and give to them His nature and characteristics.

The Conception of Colonization

There is another concept that is crucial to understanding the original purpose and plan of God for man and creation, and that is the thought that has come to be known to man as "colonization." Colonization is a process whereby a government or ruler determines to extend his kingdom, rulership, or influence to additional territory with the purpose of impacting that territory with his will and desires. The principle of colonization is understood in the process of transforming an extended territory to be just like the center of government from which it extended; that is, to manifest the nature and will of the ruler in the lifestyle, actions, activities, and culture of the territory.

Therefore, the foundation for appreciating God's creative motivation is to understand that His intent was to share His governing authority with His spirit children by extending His invisible heavenly Kingdom to a visible earthly realm for the purpose of colonizing that domain to be like heaven. Genesis 1:1 says, *"In the beginning God created the heavens and the earth"* (the physical universe). God ruled as King over a spacious and spectacular spiritual realm that He had already created. It was a world filled with angels who were there to serve Him and worship Him.

The Book of Genesis opens with God's activity in the creation of the physical world that would be the environment for the manifestation of His eternal purpose. His intention was to establish His Kingdom in that physical world, without having to come visibly into that world Himself. The purposes of the invisible God would be served by a visible creation that was the result of His creative genius. His plan would be carried out by creating from His own Spirit being a family of offspring who would be just like Him, created in His exact image. As His representatives they would release, establish, and implement His invisible Kingdom in the visible, natural world. This is His original purpose for creating man. It was not an accident. It was not a fluke. It came about through the planning and preparation of the great God of heaven who, through His love and wisdom, constructed this awesome plan. Man was right there in the center of the plan.

From the very beginning, God's plan for mankind centered in the fact that God desired to have a personal relationship with man and vice versa. *It was never God's plan to establish a religion.* As stated earlier, religion is a result of man's response to a deep spiritual vacuum in the recesses of his soul, for something he cannot describe or identify. The word *religion* denotes belief systems, creeds, and adherence to faith or convictions. These systems are manifested in the development of an array of traditions, rituals and cultural practices that extend from the simple to the very complicated. Every civilization throughout history cultivated forms of religion that sustained their viability as social entities and served as an outlet to address the mystical questions of life and death.

For many, religion has been and continues to be a tireless preoccupation distracting them from the unresolved fears of the human heart. The need for religion in some form is a universal phenomenon and is inherent in the human spirit. All humankind, left to themselves, will inevitably develop some form of religious practice. In many incidences, this can take the shape of systems of philosophies, theories, ideologies, a set of principles or documented convictions. Whatever the form takes, the purpose is the same—the attempt to satisfy the indescribable spiritual craving in the spirit of all mankind.

It is interesting to note that in the ancient writings of the Hebrew prophet and patriarch Moses, who chronicles the creation narrative of the physical universe and mankind, we do not find the establishment of a formal religious system or code of traditions for man to follow or practice.

THE BIRTH OF THE KINGDOM — THE SPIRIT OF DOMINION

The most powerful motivation in the heart of man is the pursuit of power. Why is the desire to control our environment and circumstances so overpowering to humanity? The answer is found in the very nature and heart of the human spirit.

Man was created to exercise power and designed to manage it. The motivating purpose for the creation of the human species was to dominat the earth and its resources, the result of the Creator's desires to extend His rulership from the supernatural realm to the physical realm. His plan and program was to do this through a family of spirit children He would call His sons. The record of this creative act is found in Genesis 1:26:

> Then God said, "Let us make man in Our image, in Our likeness, and let them rule (have dominion) over the fish of the sea and the birds of the air, over the livestock, over all the earth, and over all the creatures that move along the ground." So God created man in His own image, in the image of God He created him; male and female He created them (Gen. 1:26-27).

This statement is the first declaration of God's intent for you and me, and encompasses the total purpose, assignment, potential, passion and design of man as an entity. This statement is the key to man's natural desires, sense of purpose and fulfillment in life. There are a number of critical principles imbedded in this first mission statement of God, concerning man's creation, that must be carefully examined:

1. **Man was both *created* and *made*.** Both of these words are important and are distinctively different in the original Hebrew language. The word *created* is from the Hebrew word *bara* which means to create from nothing. And the word *make* is from the Hebrew word *asa* which means to form from something that is already created. Therefore, man is the integration of parts that were created from nothing and things that were already made. This mystery describes the production of man's spirit-being directly from the Spirit of God, thus making man a composite of the nature, attributes and characteristics of his source, which is God the Creator Himself. This truth is critical when discussing the spirit of dominion in mankind. It is also noteworthy at this point to understand that the word for "source" in the original Hebrew is the word *Abba* which we translate as "father". This is why God is considered the "father" of all mankind. He sourced us all and thus we possess His nature and likeness.

2. **Man was made in God's image.** The word *image* here is not referring to physical likeness, but is translated from the Hebrew words *tselem* and *demut*, both meaning essential

nature, copy, characteristics, and essence. This denotes that man as a spirit being is an expression of God's moral and spiritual nature and his attributes make him "god-like," and place Him above and beyond all earthly creation. In essence, man was created by God in the god-class and was given the responsibility to exercise that quality as God's agent on earth.

3. **God created man.** This word *man* is important because it does not refer to gender as in male, but was the name given by the Creator for the species of spirits that came out of His spirit. In essence, man is plural in tense and was the name given to the spirit species. It is also essential to note that spirits have no gender and thus man is neither male nor female but pure spirit.

4. **The Creator said let "them" have dominion over the earth.** This statement is most critical and contains the secret to the transfer of power and authority from God to man, from heaven to earth, and from the unseen to the seen world. This is the foundation of divine delegation of responsibility for management and rulership over the earth to man. This is significant because the nature of God's holiness and integrity does not allow Him to violate His own words. Thus when God spoke these words, He established the conditions of His relationship to earth through mankind. He did not say let "Us" have dominion over the earth, as that would have given Him legitimate access to earth without reference to mankind; but by these words He established mankind as the only legal authority on earth, with the power of attorney to act on His behalf. Perhaps this is why God has never done anything on earth without the cooperation of a human entity and was ultimately the reason for the necessity of His entrance into the human race as a man. Consequently, Jesus—the man—made Christ—the God—legal on earth. This is the power mankind has on planet earth.

5. **Let them have dominion.** This is the most fundamental principle for understanding the nature and the desires of mankind. Here the Creator expresses clearly, emphatically,

why He created man. This statement leaves no doubt as to what motivated His creating man and His expectation man's behavior. It also establishes man's assignment and the standard of success for his existence. This word *dominion* lays the foundation for the Kingdom concept as it relates to God's purpose and plan for the human species.

6. **Over the fish of the sea, birds of the air, the livestock, earth, and all that creep upon the ground.** This statement is crucial as it defines the nature and boundaries of the rulership of mankind. It is essential to note that the human entity is not included in the context of man's domination. The implication is that God the Creator never intended man to rule over or dominate his own kind, but rather to rule the creation and resources of earth.

WHAT IS DOMINION?

In the art of human communication it is understood that successful communication is only possible when the terms and the concepts used between the subject and object of that communication are the same.

Therefore, before we proceed any further in this most important discussion and exploration of the Kingdom concept, it is necessary for us to have a fundamental understanding of the root of this concept of "dominion" as it pertains to the Kingdom concept.

The Creator's first declaration of man's purpose for creation is hidden in this word *dominion*; and for man to understand himself and his purpose, it is imperative that this word be thoroughly understood.

The words *dominion* or *rule* are synonymous and derive their meanings from the same root words. The Hebrew words from which the concept of kingdom dominion comes are rendered *mashal, mamlakah, malkut*; and the Greek derivative is the word *basileia*. The definition of these words include "to rule," "sovereignty," "to reign," "kingdom," "to master," "to be king," "royal rule," and "kingly." The term *mamlakah* also signifies the area and the people that constitute a "kingdom." It is important to note that the concept of "king" was also considered the embodiment of kingdom. The king was viewed as the "symbol" of the kingdom proper and personified the glory of the kingdom.

Therefore the definition of *dominion* can be crafted in the following way:

To be given dominion means to be established as a sovereign, kingly ruler, master, governor, responsible for reigning over a designated territory, with the inherent authority to represent and embody as a symbol, the territory, resources and all that constitutes that kingdom.

This definition should be memorized, understood and embraced by the spirit of every man if we are to understand the original purpose and will of God our Creator for our existence. With that understanding, we can appreciate the gravity of the first proclamation of God, the Creator, concerning mankind. Man was created with a dominion mandate over earth, giving him responsibility for representing the kingdom government of God on earth. Mankind is heaven's earthly agency for kingdom rulership influence. Mankind is intended to embody the nature of God on earth and serve as His divine representative in the physical world. *The creation and commissioning of man was the first introduction and establishment of the Kingdom of heaven on earth.*

KINGDOM OF KINGS

It is also vital to apprehend that God's design for heaven's earthly kingdom is totally distinct from the structure and ideology of earthly kingdoms established by men. The proclamation by the Creator in Genesis 1:26, for man to have dominion over all the earth, was given to the entire species of mankind, both male and female. This is a fundamental precept as it renders all mankind "rulers" or kings in the earth. In fact, this mandate further establishes the Creator's intent for mankind to rule not over one another, but to exercise their royal sovereignty as a "corporate kingship," responsible to master, govern, rule, control and manage the earth and its resources. Therefore all mankind is created rulers and kings; mankind is a kingdom of kings. Perhaps this is why, as we will discuss later in this book, Jesus is designated "King of kings" in the culmination of His redemptive work.

This concept is also echoed in the word of God to the entire nation of Israel through Moses when they were released from the oppression of the kingdom of Egypt under Pharaoh.

"Now if you obey Me fully and keep My covenant, then out of all nations you will be My treasured possession. Although the whole earth is Mine, you will be for Me a kingdom of priests and a holy nation." These are the words you are to speak to the Israelites (Exod. 19:5-6).

The Intent of the Original Kingdom

The intent of the establishment of God's original kingdom of kings was to extend His rulership, will and nature from heaven to earth. His desire was to manifest His glorious character, wisdom, righteous judgments and purposes in the earth realm through the administrative leadership of mankind on earth. Man was created with the gifts and divine nature to execute God's will in the earth. The ultimate goal of God the Creator was to colonize earth with heaven and establish it as a visible territory of an invisible world. His purpose was to have His will done and the heavenly kingdom come on earth just at it is in heaven.

The Loss of A Kingdom

A few years ago I watched a television documentary on the mystery of lost civilizations and cities. The narrator led us through tales of a number of well-known myths and legends such as the lost city of Atlantis and the ruins of the Mayan civilization. I was intrigued as he presented artifacts, documents, and an array of evidence attempting to construct his argument in such a way as to prove his case. As I sat there engrossed in this presentation, I could not help but think of a similar story of the very first lost kingdom, the kingdom of Adamic kings.

When God created man, please note that the first thing He gave him was His image and likeness, but the first mandate and assignment He gave man was "dominion."

Let's carefully consider the nature of this dominion mandate as recorded in Genesis 1:26-28 and its implications as to what man's original rulership did and did not involve.

- God gave man dominion over earth.

- God gave man dominion over creation and earth, not other men.

- God never gave man dominion over heaven.

- God never gave man a religion, but a relationship.

- God never promised man heaven, but earth.

To understand the loss of the Adamic Kingdom mandate, it is important to realize you cannot lose what you never had. Adam, the first royal representative of heaven's kingdom on earth, was delegated the responsibility of serving as heaven's earthly ambassador. An ambassadorial representative is only as viable and legal as his relationship with his government. Therefore, the most important relationship the first man, Adam, had on earth was with heaven. This is why the Holy Spirit of God was intimate with mankind from the beginning. His indwelling presence guaranteed constant communication and fellowship with the will, mind, intent, and purposes of God and heaven so that He could execute His government's will on earth. This relationship made the Holy Spirit of God the most important Person on earth and established Him as the key component of the Kingdom of heaven on earth. The loss or separation of man from the Holy Spirit of God would render mankind a disqualified envoy of heaven on earth, for he would not know the will or mind of the government of heaven for earth.

As we read the Genesis record of the encounter of mankind with the adversary, the devil, in chapter 3, we see that the goal of the attack was to drive man from the garden of relationship with God and heaven, resulting in the loss of the Kingdom of heaven on earth.

AN ACT OF TREASON

Perhaps the greatest crime committed in any kingdom or nation, ancient or modern, is the crime of treason. As a matter of fact, it is the only crime to which there is no question of receiving the death penalty. It is the ultimate act of betrayal.

When a government confers on any citizen the authority and right to represent its interests, it has given the greatest form of trust possible and should be esteemed as the highest of honors. The higher the representation, the greater the responsibility and trust, and thus, the greater the influence one can have in one's nation or kingdom. This is especially critical in the context of kingdoms, where the king not only represents himself, but embodies and symbolizes the entire kingdom and all it constitutes. Adam, in essence, embodied heaven's government on earth.

Therefore, the fall of man was not just a personal act of disobedience, but was essentially an act of treason. Adam and his descendants committed the ultimate act of betrayal, deserving the penalty of death. In effect, Adam declared independence from his kingdom government, the empire of heaven, and in so doing severed his relationship with the King of heaven, abandoned his position as ambassador, and lost his dominion over earth. Through abdication of his responsibility as king over earth, Adam lost the most important relationship of all—the Holy Spirit. Through violation of God's word, mankind was rendered a disqualified representative of heaven on earth. When Adam fell through this act of treason, he did not only lose his personal relationship with his heavenly Father, but he lost a kingdom. Adam became an ambassador without portfolio, an envoy without official status, a citizen without a country, a king without a kingdom, a ruler without a domain.

A KINGDOM PROMISED

In understanding kingdoms and the concept of colonization, the success of colonization depends on the direct and uninterrupted relationship with and the submission of the colony to the imperial kingdom. The loss of the Kingdom of heaven on earth was considered rebellion against the eternal imperial Kingdom of heaven and the creating of a vagabond state. Earth became a territory under an illegal government. While Adam committed high treason, the instigator and adversary, the evil one, executed an earthly coup. Remember, Adam did not lose heaven when he fell; rather, he lost earth and dominion over earth. He lost legal representation of heaven on earth. Adam defected.

This is what God meant when he said in Genesis 2:17:

but you must not eat from the tree of the knowledge of good and evil, for when you eat of it you will surely die.

This death was not referring primarily to physical death, though that would be the ultimate result, but rather to man's spiritual disconnection from his source and kingdom. This is evidenced by the fact that Adam lived 930 years after the act of disobedience. Therefore, death to the Creator was disconnection and independence from God and the Kingdom of heaven. Adam lost the kingdom. The consequences of this rebellion were numerous:

- Loss of position and disposition;
- Transfer of responsibility;
- Self-consciousness and shame;
- Fear and intimidation of authority;
- The loss of domination over nature;
- Frustrated toil and hatred of labor;
- Pain and discomfort; and,
- The need for human accountability.

However, God's most significant response to this defection and treacherous act was His promise to the adversary recorded in Genesis 3:15-16:

And I will put enmity between you and the woman, and between your offspring and hers; he will crush your head, and you will strike his heel.

The heart of this promise is the coming of an "offspring" through a woman who would break the power of the adversary over mankind and regain the authority and dominion Adam once held, and through a process of conflict, restore the Kingdom back to mankind. This was the first promise of a messiah-king and the return of the Kingdom. Therefore, the greatest need of man was identified by what he lost; he did not lose a religion or heaven, but rather a kingdom. In God's restoration and redemptive program, heaven would not be His primary focus or goal for man, but rather the redemption, restoration and re-establishment of His Kingdom on earth. This would be the principle purpose and assignment of the promised Messiah.

Ever since this tragic cosmic calamity of man's rebellion against his heavenly kingdom government, religion has been his vain attempt to return to God's presence or to compensate for the loss. Therefore, religion represents every activity of mankind in its self-centered search for God and the kingdom, whether through Scientology, Bahai, Islam, Buddhism, Confucianism, Hinduism, Shintoism, animism, Unitarianism, atheism, or any other "ism" or philosophy. The principle motivation is to rediscover and receive what he lost, the Kingdom of God. No matter what name they bear, all religions are an exercise in futility because they express man vain frustrating pursuit to recover what he lost.

Humanity faced an insoluble dilemma: no matter how hard we tried, we could never find an infinite God by using finite human resources called religion. Fortunately for us, God solved the problem Himself, because He is the only one who could. Mankind's problem did not take God by surprise. In His omniscience—His all-knowing nature—God knew before time began that we would never find Him without His help. Therefore, God launched a journey. He set out to find *us*. God is the chaser and we are the pursued. Instead of allowing us to expend our lives in continual frustration trying to reach up and touch Him, He came down to take hold of us. His desire and purpose were to bring us back into relationship with Himself and return to us the lost Kingdom.

Religion, therefore, is simply man's search for God. No matter how committed, dedicated, loyal, faithful, zealous, active or complex our religious pursuit may be, as long as man is still searching, dissatisfied and desirous for more, he has not yet found the Kingdom. He is like a fish out of water. No matter what he does, there is only one solution to his problem. This emptiness cannot be substituted with oil, gasoline, orange juice, milk or alcohol. Religion is man's substitute for the Kingdom and that is why it cannot and will never satisfy him. Only the Kingdom can solve man's eternal problem.

I personally understand the frustration of religion. I know what it is to grow up in religion just like the Muslim, Hindu, Buddhist and all the others. I understand the dedication, loyalty and daily preoccupation with the rituals, traditions, forms and activities of religious behavior. From a child I was cultured to embrace religion and not question why we did what we were told or commanded to do. It has become plain to me now that religion preoccupies you in order to distract you—to distract you from your hunger and emptiness for the Kingdom. In essence, religion is designed to keep you too busy to fill your assignment for the Kingdom. Perhaps this is why religion has so many activities related to it. Religion is hard work and its work is its reward.

Perhaps with this understanding now the words of Jesus Christ can be understood

> *Blessed are the poor in spirit, for theirs is the kingdom of heaven. Blessed are those who mourn, for they will be comforted. Blessed are the meek, for they will inherit the earth. Blessed are those who hunger and thirst for righteousness, for they will be filled* (Matt. 5:3-6).

In His first official presentation of His message to mankind over two thousand years ago, Jesus unveiled and announced the problem and solution for mankind's dilemma in these simple statements. He identified the truth that all humanity is spiritually "poor," which means that they have a natural lack and an inherent need. He declared that the solution is not a religion but "the Kingdom." He further recognized that the whole family of mankind is in perpetual "mourning" as if something died or was lost, and He saw the coming of the "Kingdom" as the comfort to this mourning. His reference to the hunger of all mankind for "righteousness" was simply a recognition that their right relationship and right positioning, with the authority or government, is guaranteed to be satisfied by the Kingdom.

One day I sat on a stone bench in Israel right outside the famous Church of the Resurrection in Jerusalem and observed thousands of Christian pilgrims, cameras in hand, eyes filled with excitement, file into this lavishly decorated building. I had just left the place of the Temple Mount where I observed scores of Muslim pilgrims kneeling on the concrete floor of the terrace, some washing their bodies in ritual fashion at the holy water taps around the Mosque. Just below was a scene right out of history as thousands of Jewish pilgrims and worshippers rocked back and forth with such fervor that it looked painful. As I watched with interest these very beautiful activities, I could not but wonder, *Could this be what a loving God of creation enjoys?* It looked like hard work and labor. Everyone seemed to be so pressured to please some deity with the zeal of a possessed spirit. Can this really be what God desires?

Suddenly, while pondering these thoughts deep within my soul I heard the following words echoing loudly in my head:

> *Come to Me, all you who are weary and burdened, and I will give you rest. Take My yoke upon you and learn from Me, for I am gentle and humble in heart, and you will find rest for your souls. For My yoke is easy and My burden is light* (Matt. 11:28-30).

These simple words changed my life again for they fully described what I was seeing with my eyes. Religion is hard work. We will never rest until we find the Kingdom. Religion is the toil of mankind in his search for the Kingdom.

God's Original Plan for Man

To understand the past and future of man and to appreciate the present state of man's journey through time, it is crucial to consider God's original purpose and plan for His creation. God's purpose in the beginning was to:

- Establish a family of spirit sons, not servants;
- Establish a kingdom, not a religious organization;
- Establish a kingdom of kings, not subjects;
- Establish a commonwealth of citizens, not religious members;
- Establish relationship with man, not a religion;
- Extend his heavenly government to earth; and,
- Influence earth from heaven through mankind.

Sons or Servants

Being brought up in the Bahamas in the Caribbean, a former colony of the United Kingdom of Great Britain, I understand the implications of the word *servant* and the clear distinction between a servant and a son.

Under the colonial system and a product of former slaves, the role of segregation, discrimination and prejudice had detrimental influences on my life. The obstacles were evident and manifested themselves in graphic ways that clearly placed us at a disadvantage when it came to benefits and privileges in the kingdom. As servants of the crown, we were not allowed to share the same opportunities in education, work, leisure, financial prosperity and status in society. This inequity was contrasted by the seemingly unlimited fortunate lifestyles of the sons of the masters in the kingdom. A servant is definitely not the same as a son.

A closer look at God's original plan will reveal how great a divide exists between religion and relationship. God originally intended to extend His heavenly Kingdom on earth through mankind. In this plan, *God's purpose was to establish a family of sons, not a household of servants.* Just as Scripture shows us that men are Christ's Bride, so, too, are women God's sons. In Christ we are all heirs (see Rom. 8:14). In the eighth chapter of John, Jesus makes a clear distinction between servants and sons:

> *To the Jews who had believed Him, Jesus said, "If you hold to My teaching, you are really My disciples. Then you will know the truth, and the truth will set you free." They answered Him, "We are Abraham's descendants and have never been slaves of anyone. How can you say that we shall be set free?" Jesus replied, "I tell you the truth, everyone who sins is a slave to sin. Now a slave has no permanent place in the family, but a son belongs to it forever. So if the Son sets you free, you will be free indeed"* (John 8:31-36).

Jesus said that sons are members of the family, but servants are not. From the beginning, God wanted offspring who would relate to Him in love, not slaves or "hired hands" who would obey Him out of obligation. Servants may relate to their master on a superficial level, but no intimacy or sense of family exists. Sons, on the other hand, are part of the family; they are heirs who will inherit everything that belongs to their father.

SONS, NOT SUBJECTS

God's purpose was to establish a Kingdom of sons, not subjects. This is a difficult concept for us to understand at first because, from the human perspective, the existence of a king automatically implies the existence of subjects. Subjects are people who are "subject" to the king's rule and are never considered in the same class or status as royalty. However, this is not God's plan for us. God is indeed a King, but He does not want subjects. He wants sons. He does not want to rule us, but to have a family who shares His rulership.

God's Kingdom is different from earthly kingdoms in that it has no subjects. There are no peasants in the Kingdom of God, only sons. In the Kingdom of God we are not subjects but members of the royal family. Jesus Christ, the only begotten Son of God, whom Revelation 19:16 (NLB) refers to as "King of kings and Lord of lords" is our elder Brother. Everyone in God's Kingdom is a prince or princess. There are no peasants or middle class, and no order of servants. In God's Kingdom, *everyone* is related to the King.

CITIZENS, NOT RELIGIOUS MEMBERS

In addition, *God's purpose was to establish a commonwealth of citizens, not members of a religion.* This understanding is essential to grasping the concept of the message of Jesus Christ concerning the Kingdom of heaven. As a kingdom is a government and nation, it would not have members as would a religious organization. As a matter of fact the Lord never intended that those who believe in Jesus as Messiah and King be referred to as Christians. Now, you are probably stumbling over this sentence and wondering how I could make such a statement. Here's the problem: The word *Christian* has too much baggage attached to it. It refers to a whole host of people and some of them have no connection to God's Kingdom. The word has become a "religious" term devoid of any significant meaning as it relates to the Kingdom of God. Kingdoms are built upon the concept of legalities, which extends to its citizens, offering them the rights and privileges that are guaranteed by the King.

People who adhere to some religion group, including Christians, consider themselves members of the group, which they perceive as a religious and spiritual relationship with the organization or fraternity. For instance, the term *Christian* refers to an individual who adheres to or sympathizes with the Christian faith, and is identified both inside and outside that faith as a religious entity.

However, the concept of kingdom is completely opposite to the concept of religion. A kingdom consists of a king with citizens. Citizenship is essentially a legal entity with rights and privileges protected by a constitutional commitment of the king and his government. Too many Christians are simply religious people, but citizens of the Kingdom are legal people—legal in the sense that by virtue of a spiritual birth each individual in the Kingdom has the rights and blessings of citizens of this heavenly Kingdom. *We must be delivered from our religious mindsets and have our thinking readjusted so that we can take on a regal mindset.* Religious people have no rights, but legal people do. God has always desired sons who are citizens of His Kingdom, possessing the legal right to be part of His family. Citizenship is always considered a privilege in all kingdoms and nations and is usually reserved for those born into that nation or kingdom. There are special situations where one can become a citizen through privileges extended by the governing authority, but birthright is the guaranteed form of sonship and the resulting rights of citizenship. In Jesus these precious rights are conferred to everyone who trusts in Him:

> *Yet to all who received Him, to those who believed in His name, He gave the right to become children of God—children born not of natural descent, nor of human decision or a husband's will, but born of God* (John 1:12-13).

> *But our citizenship is in heaven. And we eagerly await a Savior from there, the Lord Jesus Christ, who, by the power that enables Him to bring everything under His control, will transform our lowly bodies so that they will be like His glorious body* (Phil. 3:20-21, NIV).

The name *Christian* was originally a derogatory label given by pagans to followers of Christ, even though believers through the centuries have generally accepted the term (which literally means "little Christ") and borne it with honor. Yet the term *Christian* occurs only twice in the Scriptures (Acts 26:28-29 and 1 Peter 4:16-17).

Please let me stress that I am not denying the value or the role this identification has played in the life or the history of the Christian religion over the past 2,000 years. But my concern is the restrictive religious connotations that have detracted many people from the original purpose, message, and mission of the Kingdom of God. The term

Christian tends to mentally lock a person into a religious mold and limits the reality of the truth about the Kingdom.

The Bible refers to man's relationship to God with these phrases: *servants* (which is another word for "representative minister" as a government minister), *saints, ambassadors, sons of God, citizens of heaven, kings, God's workmanship, children of God,* and other terms of endearment, but not officially are they referred to as Christians. *Christianity* was never a term given to us by Jesus Christ nor the apostles. The term *Christian* was never to be a title nor label that we wore, but a lifestyle that we lived demonstrating the nature of "Christ-likeness." In essence, *Christian* was supposed to be a description of the culture of the Kingdom being exhibited through our lives. This is why the first believers were called Christians by the early observers of their lifestyle, their power, their boldness and their Christ-like authority.

Right or wrong, most unbelievers have a definite idea of what they think a Christian should be. If we are not careful, we can identify too strongly with their label and fall into the trap of trying to live up to their expectations. We should stop trying so hard to live like *Christians* and all of the false assumptions associated with that term, and instead work harder at living like sons and daughters of God, brothers and sisters of Christ, and citizens of the Kingdom of heaven.

RELATIONSHIP OR RELIGION

Finally, *God's purpose was to establish relationship, not religion.* As stated earlier, religion is man's search for God and the Kingdom he lost. The original plan and purpose of God was to have a family of sons that He could relate to as a father to his children. This plan was evident from the beginning and is expressed more fully in the earthly introduction of the Father by Jesus Christ Himself. A careful review of the principle set forth in the Holy Scripture, which is the constitution of the Kingdom, will reveal this constant desire for personal and intimate relationship and fellowship that God desired with all mankind. All of His actions throughout history were extensions of Himself to us, as He desired to tabernacle or dwell with man. His ultimate goal was always to restore His original place with mankind. How much more personal can one get?

This is the truth behind Jesus' parable of the prodigal son, where a young man took his inheritance early, left home, and wasted his fortune in ungodly living. Later on, destitute and hungry and reduced to feeding pigs in a sty, he decided to return home, hoping to be received by his father simply as a hired servant. Upon his arrival, however, his father greeted him with joy and open arms and restored him to his rightful place in the family (see Luke 15:11-24). The father wanted his son back, not a servant.

That's the way God is, too. He wants sons, not servants or subjects; He wants citizens, not Christians; and, He wants relationships, not religion.

RULING THE VISIBLE WORLD FROM THE INVISIBLE REALM

God's simple strategy for extending and establishing His Kingdom on this earth was to rule the visible world of man from the invisible realm of the spirit. The plan meant that man would be His visible representative created specifically to live in the visible realm to represent Him. Let me put it another way. *God's original purpose and intent was to rule that which is seen* (the visible world) *through that which is unseen* (the invisible world). *He would do this through the unseen* (the Spirit of God in man), *living in the unseen* (spirit of man) *and living in the seen* (the physical body) *on the scene* (the earth).

> *For since the creation of the world His invisible attributes, His eternal power and divine nature, have been clearly seen, being understood through what has been made, so that they are without excuse* (Rom. 1:20 NAS).

> *For by Him all things were created, both in the heavens and on earth, visible and invisible, whether thrones or dominions or rulers or authorities—all things have been created through Him and for Him* (Col. 1:16 NAS).

> *By faith we understand that the worlds were prepared by the word of God, so that what is seen was not made out of things which are visible* (Heb. 11:3 NAS).

43

How would He accomplish this? God, who is unseen, would put His Spirit into the unseen spirit of man—a spirit inhabiting a visible physical body living on the visible earth. Through man's spirit a window of the soul is created so that man can communicate with the invisible world of God and also through another window man is able to communicate through his body to the visible world of man. Man is created in such a powerful and unique way that he is exalted above all of God's creation.

By this means God could communicate from the unseen realm through the unseen spirit man to the seen realm, so that the visible world of man could understand His will. Whatever God desired would be relayed to the unseen, then manifested in the seen on the scene so that the earth would show what heaven was thinking.

KING OF THE INVISIBLE AND VISIBLE WORLDS

God, then, is the King of both the invisible and the visible realms—the spiritual world and the physical universe. He is El Shaddai, God Almighty, the Ruler who sets all the standards in heaven and earth. He lives in and rules the unseen realm and is the Creator and owner of the seen realm, where He also created human beings to rule under His authority as vice-regents of the earth. As King of everything, God is the standard setter, the rule establisher, and the Judge of all things. That's what it means to be King.

A king cannot be a king unless he has something to rule over. It is impossible to be a king over nothing. Before anything else was, God was. Yet, in the strictest sense of the word, God was not a king until He created a realm over which to rule. Until that time, He was just God—omniscient and omnipotent, Father, Son, and Holy Spirit, three-in-one, complete, whole, and self-contained—standing on nothing but by the corner of nowhere. Then, in accordance with His nature, He created first a spiritual realm and then a physical realm.

If God was fully complete within Himself, why did He create the universe and everything in it, both seen and unseen? He did it for His own pleasure and because He is by nature a Creator. Creating is His natural expression. Upon completing His creation, the Creator became King of creation because He now had a realm to rule over.

Worthy are You, our Lord and our God, to receive glory and honor and power; for You created all things, and because of Your will they existed, and were created (Rev. 4:11 NAS).

THE KING AND HIS DOMAIN

Whatever a king rules over is called his domain. Without a domain, the title "king" has little meaning and carries little weight. There can be no president without a country, no prime minister without a nation; every ruler must have a realm to rule. Unlike human rulers who obtain their domains by election, subterfuge, or conquest, God created His own domain, and He will never be unseated. There will never be a *coup d'etat* in the Kingdom of heaven.

The word *kingdom* is derived from the words "king" and "domain." A kingdom is the "king domain," the realm over which the king rules with complete sovereignty. God's "king domain" includes both the seen and unseen. The Bible says that God created all things and without Him "nothing was made that has been made" (John 1:3). Whatever God created is His property by right of creation. Since He created everything, everything belongs to Him. Therefore, His domain extends infinitely in every direction because there is nowhere on earth or in the heavens that He does not encompass or where His presence does not dwell.

MAN WAS CREATED FOR DOMINION

God is King over everything that is, whether visible or invisible. From His throne in heaven He reigns in glory and majesty over the invisible spirit realm. His reign over the physical domain takes a different form. Rather than rule directly, God chose from the very beginning to exercise His kingly authority on earth through human envoys created in His image to rule the earth in His name as His representatives.

God's purpose and plan for mankind are clearly revealed in the first chapter of Genesis:

Then God said, "Let Us make man in Our image, in Our likeness, and let them rule over the fish of the sea and the birds of the air, over the livestock, over all the earth, and over all the creatures that move along the ground." So God created man in His own image, in the image of God He created him; male and female He created them.

45

God blessed them and said to them, "Be fruitful and increase in number; fill the earth and subdue it. Rule over the fish of the sea and the birds of the air and over every living creature that moves on the ground" (Gen. 1:26-28).

God created man because He desired someone to *rule* over the physical realm He had created. The King James Version of the Bible uses the word *dominion,* which is related to the word *domain.* Human beings were created to exercise dominion over the earth and all its creatures. Earth is the domain of humanity's rulership.

May you be blessed by the Lord, the Maker of heaven and earth. The highest heavens belong to the Lord, but the earth He has given to man (Ps. 115:15-17).

A KINGDOM OF KINGS

Notice also that these verses say nothing of human beings ruling over other human beings. It was not God's original design that any man would rule other human beings. *He created all of us to rule, not to be ruled.* In accordance with His own plan, God needed someone to dominate a piece of real estate called earth, so He created man. God made us to be in charge of this unique territory, to rule over the earth domain. Many of us have either lost sight of this truth or never learned it in the first place. Understanding that we were created for dominion carries truly life-changing ramifications.

God's purposes never change. He remains committed to His plan for man to dominate this planet on His behalf. Trapped inside every one of us is a dominion spirit crying for release and a dominion mandate waiting to be exercised. It is this natural spirit of dominion that causes us to naturally rebel against any attempt to dominate or control our lives or destiny. Whether the oppression comes from religion or the world systems, humans were not meant to live a life of subjugation and will always resistoppression.

You may note that in every situation where there has been an extended reign of an oppressive regime in any nation, such as apartheid in South Africa, or the oppression of communist ideology, or the repressive government of Iran or Iraq, that when deliverance came, the people rejoiced like steam being released from a pressure cooker. The fall of Saddam Hussein's oppressive regime in Iraq, for example, was followed by thousands of Iraqis celebrating in the streets and exercising freedoms they had not enjoyed in decades. Why were they so quick to cast off the restraints of the old government? It was because they hated their oppression. We are all the same—we were not created to be dominated but to dominate in every area of our life.

At the same time, it is truly amazing how many kinds of things we allow to dominate us. We are supposed to have dominion over plants and yet look how we allow plants to run (and ruin) our lives: coca leaves from Colombia, tobacco leaves from Cuba, grape juice and grains used to make wine and liquor. Coffee, cigarettes, liquors—we are subject to all kind of vices that rule over our appetites.

We are supposed to rule our passions and desires—sex, greed, drugs, power, money, and possessions—but instead, they often rule us.

Many people live and work for money, thinking it will bring them freedom, when all along they slowly and seductively become the slaves of the things for which they work. People who properly understand finances understand that they do not work for money. The money works for them. Those who are slaves of money will never truly get ahead.

If you find that you are one of those who are working for money and are poor, you will remain poor and will never be able to get out of the economic hole in which you are living. If you are middle class, that is where you will stay. As long as you go after the money, it will elude you. As soon as you learn to make money work for you, it will come back to you multiplied many times over.

One of the first things that happened to the early Church in the Book of Acts was directly related to the entire issue of dominion.

All the believers were one in heart and mind. No one claimed that any of his possessions was his own, but they shared everything they had. With great power the apostles continued to testify to the resurrection of the Lord Jesus, and much grace was upon them all. There were no needy persons among them. For from time to time those who owned lands or houses sold them, brought the money from the sales and put it at the apostles' feet, and it was distributed to anyone as he had need (Acts 4:32-35).

The main point I would like to note here is that they brought their monies and laid it at the feet of the apostles. This established the principle that the master of money that once dominated them now had to bow and become a slave to the Kingdom of God. By the very act of sharing their possessions with one another and by selling houses and land and giving the money from the sale to be distributed to others as needed, these early believers were exercising dominion over that which had previously dominated them. In Christ they found the freedom to rule as they had been created to do, rather than to be ruled by their own uncontrolled desires. Money did not have a hold on them. They had a hold on the money. In his first letter to the believers in Corinth, Paul expressed perfectly what our attitude should be in this regard: *"'Everything is permissible for me—but I will not be mastered by anything"* (1 Cor. 6:12b).

God's "Management Contract" with Man

At creation, God gave man dominion over the entire physical realm, making him the de facto king of the earth. To *dominate* means "to govern, rule, control, manage, lead, or have authority over something." There is a very important distinction here. God gave us *rulership* of the earth, not ownership. Someone who gives up ownership to another person also surrenders all responsibility for it. The person who assigns the position of rulership of a place but retains ownership, will retain the ultimate responsibility. That is why God set up a qualification from the start. He told Adam, *"As long as you obey Me and do not eat the fruit of the tree at the center of the garden, you can manage this planet all you want, for as long as you want; it's yours"* (see Gen. 2:16-17).

In the beginning, God gave us a "management contract" or a "lease agreement," of sorts. The Bible is very clear that the earth belongs to God. Psalm 24:1 says, *"The earth is the Lord's, and everything in it, the world, and all who live in it."* God owns the earth, but He gave it to us to manage under a lease agreement that we could call a *dominion mandate*. Under this mandate we must give to God, the owner, an accounting of what we do with that which He has entrusted to us. He will judge us according to how well we manage His assets.

Jesus taught this principle in His parable about a master who entrusted a sum of money to each of three servants and then went on a long journey. While he was gone, two of the servants invested the money wisely and received a double return. The third servant did nothing except hide his allotment. Upon the master's return, He commended the two servants who had exercised wise management. He rewarded them with increased privilege and responsibility. However, He cast out the servant who shirked the responsibility of stewardship (see Matt. 25:14-30).

BORN TO RULE, NOT TO BE RULED

We were born to rule the earth—all of us. When we do not become who we were meant to be or fulfill our destiny, we open the door to a whole world of personal problems. Allowing ourselves to be dominated by our physical environment or by other people can result in things like high blood pressure and other physical problems and illnesses. It can even open the door to mental and emotional troubles. One of the most liberating events of my life happened to me as a teenager. It was the day I discovered my Kingdom dominion mandate for my life. Psalm 115 states it perfectly:

> *May the Lord make you increase, both you and your children. May you be blessed by the Lord, the Maker of heaven and earth. The highest heavens belong to the Lord, but the earth He has given to man* (Ps. 115:14-16).

Verse 16 is an awesome verse. The phrase "the highest heavens" refers to the heavens above the stratosphere—the invisible world where God lives. Heaven is God's realm, but He gave the earth to man, not in a deed of ownership, but as a lease agreement of proprietorship. Here the Bible tells us directly that heaven is not our territory.

Believers often talk about going to heaven when they die. Although that is true, God has made arrangements to make sure that we don't stay there. If we stayed in heaven, God's Word would fail, because He has plainly stated that He created us to have dominion over the earth. God's Word can never fail:

As the rain and the snow come down from heaven, and do not return to it without watering the earth and making it bud and flourish, so that it yields seed for the sower and bread for the eater, so is My word that goes out from My mouth: It will not return to Me empty, but will accomplish what I desire and achieve the purpose for which I sent it (Isa. 55:10-11).

If God says He created us to exercise dominion over the earth, then clearly we cannot stay in heaven. God's purpose for us has always been that we dominate the earth. Our tendency in the Church is to over-focus on heaven. The King of the universe has given us an earthly mandate. That is why He has made arrangements to ensure that believers who die now will return to the earth with the Lord. God has even made arrangements for our new bodies: It's called the resurrection.

THE LAW OF THE KING: MAN SHALL MANAGE PLANET EARTH

By God's design and intention, we have dominion over the earth. This means that we are the managers, supervisors, rulers, governors, leaders, and stewards of this planet. Whatever happens here is our responsibility. God will hold us accountable for our stewardship. Our authority in this realm is so complete that God Himself will not violate it. Now I know that this statement will cause some of you to wonder how I could make such a bold assertion. Isn't God sovereign and can't He do whatever He wants? In theory that is true, but just as the word of an earthly king is law and cannot be reversed, so the word of the King of the universe is law and cannot change. At this point let us take a look at one of the most important principles in the constitution of the Word of God concerning your creation and the program of God for your rulership-strategy on earth. In the Book of Genesis we have already seen that God established the law that man was granted absolute responsibility for the earth realm. Man was commissioned to rule over all of God's creation. He was given the will, the wisdom, and the authority to carry out this command.

Then God said, "Let Us make man in Our image, in Our likeness, and let them rule over the fish of the sea and the birds of the air, over the livestock, over all the earth, and over all the creatures that move along the ground" (Gen. 1:26).

Two of the most important words ever spoken by the Creator are locked away in this verse, and they establish the nature of the relationship God desired with the earth realm. Those words are "let them." By these words the Creator God established a law which gives only to mankind the legal authority to exercise dominion and control over earth. It is interesting to note that God did not say "let Us" but rather "let them." If He had said "let Us," then He would have provided access by Himself to earth anytime without violating His word and thus be co-ruler with man on the earth. But by stating "let them," He locked Himself out of the earth as a spirit being without a body.

Why is this so important to understand? Because God is a spirit and when He speaks, His words become law. His integrity will not permit Him to violate or break His word; therefore, whatever He speaks becomes a law even unto God. He will never break His word nor violate His principles.

In this case, the result is that God in His sovereignty has decided to delegate authority and dominion in the earth to mankind—a spirit in a body. This is why God cannot do anything on earth without the cooperation of a human. Man is God's legal agency and access to earth.

God is and remains absolutely sovereign, but He has chosen to limit His activity or intervention on the earth to that which we, the proprietors, give Him permission to do. The way we grant that permission is through prayer.

I offer you two biblical stories that illustrate my premise. The first comes from an event that happened in ancient Babylon. In the sixth chapter of Daniel, King Darius of the Medes and Persians was seduced by evil men to make a king's decree. The king issued a statute and established a law that no one could petition any other god or he would be thrown into a den of hungry lions. It is important that kings consider carefully their decrees and the implications of those decrees because once they are made they cannot be reversed.

Now, O king, establish the injunction and sign the document so that it may not be changed, according to the law of the Medes and Persians, which may not be revoked (Dan. 6:8, NAS).

We all know the story very well. There was no way that Daniel could submit to this decree and was caught in the action of worshiping the God of Israel. When King Darius found out, he was *deeply distressed* and set out to save Daniel from his own decree. In the end, there was nothing he could do. It was the law of the king and could not be reversed even by the king himself.

The second story comes from the New Testament. Because of John the Baptist's fiery condemnation of King Herod's relationship with his brother's wife, Herod had him arrested and put in prison. Herodias conspired against John and devised an evil scheme. Herodias' daughter appeared at King Herod's birthday party and danced very seductively before Herod and his guests. At the end of the dance, in a drunken state of seduction, Herod offered her anything she wanted, but he was stunned by her response as the young maiden asked for the head of John. Herod was grieved and overwhelmed but he knew he was trapped. He had made a decree and it could not be reversed.

GOD NEEDS A BODY

This law of divine delegation creating human dominion over earth has made the body of man indispensable and a prerequisite for legal activity on earth. This is why God's Spirit could not stop the fall of man, not because He was weak, powerless or impotent, but rather because He was faithful to His word. The fall of man, therefore, is in essence a result of the faithfulness of God. However, this is also why the promise of the Kingdom being taken from the adversary had to include and required the promise of the coming of the Spirit of God in a human body.

Bound by His own law, Father already had a plan worked out. He would introduce His own Son into the human equation. By the power of incarnation God would circumvent His own law. Through Jesus, God could accomplish His will. Throughout the life of Jesus we see His commitment to the will of the Father.

Jesus therefore answered and was saying to them, "Truly, truly, I say to you, the Son can do nothing of Himself, unless it is something He sees the Father doing; for whatever the Father does, these things the Son also does in like manner." So Jesus said, "When you lift up the Son of Man, then you will know that I am He, and I do nothing on My own initiative, but I speak these things as the Father taught Me" (John 5:19; 8:28 NAS).

God needs a body to get His will done on earth. Through Jesus He got that body and now through the indwelling of Christ in us He can continue that work. During Jesus' earthly ministry He offered us various secret keys of the Kingdom. One of those keys is the power of prayer. By the power of prayer we can arrange to get God's power into our earthly realm.

Jesus told His disciples:

I tell you the truth, whatever you bind on earth will be bound in heaven, and whatever you loose on earth will be loosed in heaven. Again, I tell you that if two of you on earth agree about anything you ask for, it will be done for you by My Father in heaven. For where two or three come together in My name, there am I with them (Matt. 18:18-20).

What Jesus said to His disciples applies equally to all believers. When it comes to things in the earthly realm, heaven responds to what we do. Heaven binds what we bind and looses what we loose. In other words, God will not do anything on earth without permission or access from those on earth to whom He gave dominion. So if something we want to see on the earth is not happening, it is because we are not allowing it to happen. Prayer is important because it is our means of constantly granting God permission to "interfere" in the affairs of men on earth. God *can* do anything, but because He has given us the license, He can release on the earth only what we allow.

Augustine, an early Church Father, once wrote, *"Without God we cannot, without us God will not."*[1] This is a concise description of how our dominion mandate works. Without God's power and Spirit, we have no chance of affecting the earth for the Kingdom of heaven. Without our agreement and permission through prayer, God will not interfere. But through His Son, the Lord Jesus, and then subsequently through the Body of Christ, God can intervene. In His sovereignty, God has seen to it that there have always been people on the earth who agree with His purpose and plan and through whom He can obtain access in order to accomplish His divine purposes in the earthly realm.

If we want God to keep on interfering, we need to keep on praying. Prayer is serious business. When we pray we are communicating with a divine government for whom we are ambassadors. Prayer is the medium through which we get our "faxes," "e-mails," and flow of information and resources from heaven, and through which God's government gains access to act on the earth according to our faith and dominion authority.

A FALL SHOOK THE WORLD

God created mankind for dominion over the earth, but the fall of man disrupted and sabotaged that program. When Adam and Eve disobeyed God, they fell not from heaven but from dominion. Satan deceived Eve by promising her that if she ate from the fruit of the tree of the knowledge of good and evil (the tree God had placed off limits), her eyes would be opened and she would become like God. The problem was, she *already* was like God. She and Adam were created in God's image, and their power and authority in the earthly realm mirrored God's in the heavenly realm.

The greatest weapon anyone can use against us is self-doubt. Satan used this weapon against Eve. By causing her to doubt herself, he opened the door for her to begin doubting God as well. Self-doubt involves low self-esteem, a negative self-concept, and a low sense of personal worth and value. If this is the way we see ourselves, it can lead us to doubt the character and qualities of the God who (we suppose) made us that way.

With this kind of mindset, it is no surprise that we end up thinking of ourselves as doubters rather than believers, losers rather than winners, followers rather than leaders, and subjects rather than sons. We have been so conditioned by our past, our culture, and our environment that we have lost sight of who we really are. Instead of taking our seat at the family dinner table, we content ourselves with eating in the servants' quarters because we believe that is all we are entitled to. Our attitude should be that no matter where we are right now or what are our current circumstances, eventually we are going to be in charge. What we need is an entirely new mentality.

I will never forget one meeting in Malaysia where I spoke to a group of executives with the Sony company. During a meal I was chatting with some of them—these were all high-powered individuals, every one of them a multimillionaire—when one told me the story of how he made his fortune. This individual was a Chinese gentleman who was in Malaysia as a consultant with Sony. After sharing his story with me, he asked, "Can you tell me why it is that people of your particular pigmentation, no matter what country they reside in, generally do not quite break through to true financial success? We Chinese usually make money wherever we go." He was not at all vain or arrogant with his question, but was simply inquiring about an observation he had made in his travels.

"I really don't know," I replied. "Can you tell me?"

He answered by saying, "During a trip to America, I noticed in every city I visited that when an Asian comes to town, even if he has nothing when he starts, he owns a business in just a few months. People of your pigmentation, on the other hand, even though most of them are very hard working, have been there for decades, yet most often do not own anything. After studying this for a while and talking to many of your people, I finally figured out that *the difference lies not in our abilities, but in our mentalities.* More often than not, when your people go into a city, they go looking for a job. It is different with Asians. We Chinese never look for jobs. When we go into a city, we are looking for a *business.* We may need to hold a job for a while, but that is only until we can buy or start a business of our own."

Building a Kingdom Mentality

It all comes down to whether or not we have a *Kingdom mentality.* If you believe that you are supposed to follow all the time, then follow on; the world is full of people who will be more than happy to lead you. If, however, you detect the seed of leadership in you, if you see evidence of the dominion mandate in your spirit and commit yourself to follow it, nothing can stop you. That mandate is inside every one of us, for God put it there.

Long ago, at the age of 14, I decided that no one on earth was born to rule over me; only God had that right and authority. He alone was qualified. Some people have observed that attitude in me and called it arrogance. I am not arrogant; I simply understand my rights and privileges as a Kingdom citizen.

As children of God and sinners saved by the blood of Jesus, we have no reason to feel ashamed of who we are or to sell ourselves short. Instead, we should embrace our identity as beings created in the image of God. We are like our Father, and we should live accordingly, boldly claiming our rights as citizens of a heavenly Kingdom. There is no reason for us to walk around with our heads down and our shoulders drooped.

There should be confidence in our demeanor and a spring in our step. We are children of the King! His Kingdom belongs to us as well. Jesus said, *"Do not be afraid, little flock, for your Father has been pleased to give you the kingdom"* (Luke 12:32). God gave us dominion over the earth, an awesome responsibility as well as a wonderful privilege. Let us not conduct ourselves like vagabonds, servants, or hired hands who have no personal interest or stake in the land, but as wise children giving careful and confident management of a realm that we stand to inherit one day.

THE RULERS BECOME THE RULED

When Adam and Eve disobeyed God, they did not lose heaven, but gave up their kingdom on earth. By listening to satan they committed high treason and surrendered their ruling authority. By abdicating their throne of dominion, they subjected all humans of succeeding generations to subjugation as slaves of the enemy. *They who should have been deployed became employed by an evil taskmaster.* The rulers became the ruled, the victors the victims, and the kings the subjects.

Jesus told the parable of the prodigal son to explain to us what happened and to reveal the Father's attitude toward us. God stands ready to welcome us home with open arms to completely restore our full status as sons and daughters. Our problem is that too often we accept only the contract that the prodigal son wanted—to be a servant in his father's house.

We want to be servants of the Lord, and although that is certainly what we are as believers, there is so much more to our relationship than that. If we settle for just being His servants, we will miss out on much of the joy of knowing Christ and the fullest and deepest aspects of Kingdom living. Too many of God's people only know how to be "workers in the field" and don't know what it means to be a "son in the house."

Jesus said, "I no longer call you servants, because a servant does not know his master's business. Instead, I have called you friends, for everything that I learned from My Father I have made known to you" (John 15:15). *Jesus Christ is our Savior by circumstance, but our elder Brother by a natural/spiritual genealogy.*

Hebrews 2:11 says, "Both the One who makes men holy and those who are made holy are of the same family. So Jesus is not ashamed to call them brothers." So often, however, we tend to relate to Him as our Savior much more than as our big Brother.

Many people in today's world, including many believers, are in a plight similar to that of the prodigal son, whose mentality was damaged by his time in the pigpen. Like him, they come from an environment that makes it difficult to believe that they can ever become sons or daughters again. Here is God's glorious truth: All people on earth—no matter who they are, where they live, or what they have done—are *potential* children of God and Kingdom citizens. Lost children are still children. That is why the gospel of the Kingdom is such good news; it is a message sent from Daddy to all His children telling them that they can return home to the Kingdom and once again be sons and daughters in their full right.

Upon his son's return, the father in Jesus' parable called first for a ring to be put on his son's hand. The ring was the symbol of sonship and authority in the family. Once the young man had the ring, it meant that everything else in his father's house was his as well. Christ came to earth, died on the cross, and rose from the dead to put a ring of sonship on everyone's finger to bring us back into fellowship with our Father so that we might assume our rightful place as His children and as citizens in His Kingdom.

For many of us, taking that step will require first a change or renewing of our minds to get rid of "pigpen thinking." Consider Paul's words to the Roman believers:

> *Therefore, I urge you, brothers, in view of God's mercy, to offer your bodies as living sacrifices, holy and pleasing to God—this is your spiritual act of worship. Do not conform any longer to the pattern of this world, but be transformed by the renewing of your mind. Then you will be able to test and approve what God's will is—His good, pleasing and perfect will* (Rom. 12:1-2, NIV).

SAVED, BUT NOT CONVERTED

Even though Paul was addressing believers—people who had placed their faith and trust in Jesus Christ as Savior and Lord—many of his readers still needed to undergo a change of mindset. Although they were children of God by faith, they were still caught up in a "pigpen" mentality of thinking like slaves.

This is a truth we need to consider carefully today. It is possible for a person to be "saved" but not "converted." Salvation takes place instantly; it is a spiritual transaction in which our sins are cleansed by the blood of Jesus as we trust Him in faith.

Conversion, on the other hand, can take a lifetime as we learn how to think, live, and act as children of God. It is like moving suddenly from a dilapidated shack into a mansion; we bring all our old habits and "shack" mentality with us, and they change only gradually over time.

When Paul says that we should "offer [our] bodies as living sacrifices," he is telling us to bring our bodies under management—to get them under control. Stop drinking or stealing or smoking or lying or doing drugs. Stop engaging in illicit and immoral sexual activity. Stop playing around with pornography. Break off unhealthy relationships. Bring our bodies under subjection. Keep our bodies and minds pure.

It is important that we learn to manage our body and get it in order because it is our legal house. If we lose it, we cannot do anything else. We can't serve God effectively if we are addicted to tobacco or alcohol. We can't fulfill our potential if by age 30 we are sick and have cancer in our lungs. The Lord cannot bless us if we are shacking up with someone or abusing our minds or bodies in any way, or living in any manner that is contrary to His revealed will. He wants us to bring our bodies under subjection and present them to Him as *living* sacrifices from which He can receive great glory and honor.

A Change of Mind

Paul says next that we need to "be transformed by the renewing of [our] mind." What does he mean? His point is that even though as believers we have been born again, we still have a mental problem. We have the Holy Spirit, but not the *spirit* of the Holy Spirit. We have the anointing but not the *spirit* of the anointing. We need to change our thinking. The Greek word *metamorphoo* (from which comes the English word *metamorphosis*) literally means "to make a complete and total change." The transformation that Paul talks about here involves a complete revolution of our mental state.

I had to fight this fight, too. For a long time after I became a believer, I loved God but complained because life in general seemed so terrible. I knew God was good, but wondered why everything bad seemed to be happening to me. It seemed as though wicked people all around me were making it and enjoying life and moving ahead, while I was stuck. I prayed and I fasted and believed God for the best, but things never seemed to change. Finally, I asked in despair, "God, what's wrong here?"

"There's nothing wrong with those wicked people," He answered. "They are simply sons and daughters who do not yet know their Father. As for you, your problem is that although you are saved, you are mentally damaged."

I had to learn how to change my thinking, to think not like a loser and a nobody, but like a winner and a son of the Father. That's what Paul is saying to all of us. We must learn to think like kings again, to lay hold of the spirit and attitude of kings. This is why Kingdom citizenship is really all about leadership. It is about kingship and ruling a domain. It is not about being low, humble, and poor in the false, demeaning way that so many of us think. Kingdom citizenship is about recognizing our place and rights through Christ as citizens of God's Kingdom, and claiming those rights so that we can fulfill God's Kingdom purpose in our world. It is about taking over again that which once was lost because of our sin and disobedience. Our Kingdom faith is about claiming and living out our *dominion mandate*.

[1]Commonly attributed to St. Augustine, as cited by Dr. William Schwein, "Toward 2000: Giving God His Job Description," Nov. 21, 1999, from http://www.carmelumc.org/ser mons/Serm_991121.htm.

PRINCIPLES

1. God's original plan in creation was to extend His heavenly Kingdom on earth.

2. God's purpose was to establish a family of sons, not servants.

3. God's purpose was to establish a Kingdom of sons, not subjects.

4. God's purpose was to establish a commonwealth of citizens, not Christians.

5. God's purpose was to establish relationships, not religion.

6. God's original purpose and intent was to rule the seen from the unseen through the unseen living in the seen on the scene.

7. Human beings were created to exercise dominion over the earth and all its creatures.

8. God gave us rulership of the earth, not ownership.

9. God will not do anything on earth without permission or access from those on earth to whom He gave dominion.

10. God can do anything, but because He has given us the license, He can release on the earth only what we allow.

11. The gospel of the Kingdom is good news: a message sent from Daddy to all His children telling them that they can return home to the Kingdom and once again be sons and daughters in their full right.

"*The future of mankind
is in his past.*"

REDISCOVERING
THE KINGDOM CONCEPT

At the beginning of this book we talked about the power and importance of concepts when attempting to understand and communicate our ideas. It is most important to note that God the Creator chose the concept of a kingdom to communicate His purpose, will and plan for mankind and earth to us. The message of the Bible is primarily and obviously about a Kingdom. If you do not understand kingdoms, it is impossible for you to understand the Bible and its message.

However, over the past 2,000 years the true concept of kingdom has been lost, especially since the advent of modern governments built on new concepts of governing, e.g., democracy, socialism, communism, and dictatorships.

For the most part, people in the Western world know very little about kingdom and the concept of royalty and monarchy.

This is further compounded by the idea that kingdoms are designed to elevate one family above all families and subjugate and oppress citizens. While it is true that many kingdoms have dark histories of atrocities and oppression, prospering at the expense of the dignity and value of their citizens, the original concept of kingdom as introduced by God Himself, stands alone as the perfect prototype of government built on righteous judgment. All the kingdoms of the earth were mere attempts to imitate this perfect Kingdom. Today our modern democracies are attempts to achieve the goals of the perfect kingdom, without the necessary raw material—the Holy Spirit.

Added to this confusion, and even ignorance, concerning kingdom, religion has further diverted our understanding by converting the message of the Kingdom of God into a moral belief system. The result is that religion has become an end in itself, distinguishing itself from the Kingdom concept with pride. In fact, many religions take pride in the separation of religion and state and see the two as opposing entities with no common relationship. The dilemma is that the Kingdom is a state government with all the characteristics of a state.

Jesus came to earth to restore what Adam lost, and He brought a kingdom message. Jesus came to reestablish the government of God on earth and to reinstate His earthly kings to their rightful place of dominion. Adam lost a kingdom, not a religion, and therefore the redemptive work of the Creator would be the reestablishment of His Kingdom on earth. Let's take a look at what a Kingdom entails, in order to better understand the message of Jesus Christ and the Bible.

WHAT IS A KINGDOM?

The kingdom concept was born in the heart of man, placed there by his Creator as the purpose for which he was created. Despite the fact that there were many types of kingdoms throughout history, there are certain characteristics common to all kingdoms. The Kingdom of God, according to Jesus, also possesses these components. Here are some you will need to know in order to understand the concepts of Scripture.

All kingdoms have:

- A King and Lord – a sovereign;
- A Territory – a domain;
- A Constitution – a royal covenant;
- A Citizenry – community of subjects;
- Law – acceptable principles;
- Privileges – rights and benefits;
- A Code of Ethics – acceptable lifestyle and conduct;
- An Army – security; and,
- A Commonwealth – economic security; and,
- A Social Culture – protocol and procedures.

The King is the embodiment of the kingdom, representing its glory and nature. Authority flows from the king and the word of the king is supreme.

The Territory is the domain over which the king exercises total authority. The territory and its resources and people are all personal property of the king. The king by right owns all and, therefore, is considered lord over all. The word *Lord* denotes ownership by right. *Lord* is only given to one who is sovereign owner. This is why the Scriptures declare, *"The earth is the Lord's and the fullness thereof; the world, and they that dwell therein."* (Ps. 24:1 KJV).

The Constitution is the covenant of a king with his citizenry and expresses the mind and will of the king for his citizens and the kingdom. It constitutes the intent of the sovereign for his people as well as containing the benefits and privileges of the kingdom. The constitution is the documented words of the king. The Bible contains the constitution of the Kingdom of God which details His will and mind for His citizens.

The Citizenry is the people that live under the rule of the king. Citizenship in a kingdom is not a right, but a privilege, and is a result of the king's choice. The benefits and privileges of a kingdom are only accessible to citizens and, therefore, the favor of the king is always a privilege. Once one becomes a citizen of the kingdom, all the rights of citizenship are at the citizen's pleasure. The king is obligated to care for and protect all of his citizens, and their welfare is a reflection on the king himself. The number one goal of a citizen in a kingdom is to submit to the king, seeking only to remain in right standing with him. This is called righteousness. This is why Jesus said the priority of all men is to seek His kingdom.

But seek first His kingdom and His righteousness, and all these things will be given to you as well (Matt. 6:33).

The Law constitutes the standards and principles established by the king himself, by which his kingdom will function and be administered. The laws of a kingdom are to be obeyed by all, including foreigners residing in it. The laws of a kingdom are the way by which one is guaranteed access to the benefits of the king and the kingdom. Violations of kingdom law places one at odds with the king and thus interrupts the favorable position one enjoys with the king. The laws in a kingdom cannot be changed by the citizens, nor are they subject to a citizen referendum or debate. Simply put, the word of the king is law in His kingdom. Rebellion against the law is rebellion against the king. King David understood this principle of the royal word when he stated,

> *I will bow down toward Your holy temple and will praise Your name for Your love and Your faithfulness, for You have exalted above all things Your name and Your word (Ps. 138:2-3).*

The Privileges are the benefits the king lavishes on his faithful citizens. This aspect of kingdom is very different from other forms of government. In a kingdom, citizenship is always desired by the people because, once you are in the kingdom, the king is personally responsible for you and all your needs. In addition, because the king owns everything within his kingdom, he can give to any citizen any or all of his wealth as he desires.

A Code of Ethics is the acceptable conduct of the citizens in the kingdom and their representation of the kingdom. This code includes moral standards, social relationships, personal conduct, attitude, attire and manner of life.

The Army is the kingdom's system of securing its territory and protecting its citizens. It is important to understand that in a kingdom the citizens do not fight in the army, but enjoy the protection of the army. This is why, in the Kingdom of God, the angels are called the host of heaven. This word *host* means army and identifies the angels as the so-called military component of the Kingdom of heaven. This kingdom concept presents a challenge to our religious thinking of the Church as an army. A careful study of the biblical constitution of the word will show that the Church, as Jesus established it, is not identified as an army but rather a citizenship, a family of sons and a nation.

> *He unleashed against them His hot anger, His wrath, indignation and hostility—a band of destroying angels (Ps. 78:49-50).*

> *Praise the Lord, you His angels, you mighty ones who do His bidding, who obey His word. Praise the Lord, all His heavenly hosts, you His servants who do His will (Ps. 103:20-21).*

So it will be at the end of the age. The Son of Man will send out His angels, and they will weed out of His kingdom everything that causes sin and all who do evil. They will throw them into the fiery furnace, where there will be weeping and gnashing of teeth (Matt. 13:40b-42).

A Commonwealth is the economic system of a kingdom which guarantees each citizen equal access to financial security. In a kingdom, the term *commonwealth* is used because the king's desire is that all his citizens share and benefit from the wealth of the kingdom. The kingdom's glory is in the happiness and health of its citizens.

Consider carefully the word of the King of the Kingdom of God, Jesus Christ,

Then Jesus said to His disciples: "Therefore I tell you, do not worry about your life, what you will eat; or about your body, what you will wear. Life is more than food, and the body more than clothes (Luke 12:22-24).

But seek His kingdom, and these things will be given to you as well. Do not be afraid, little flock, for your Father has been pleased to give you the kingdom (Luke 12:31-32).

The Social Culture is the environment created by the life and manners of the king and his citizens. This is the cultural aspect that separates and distinguishes the kingdom from all others around it. It is the culture that expresses the nature of the king, through the lifestyle of his citizens. This distinction in Kingdom culture is evidenced in the words of the Lord Jesus, when He repeatedly said in the Book of Matthew, *"you have heard it said... but I tell you,"* (Matt. 5:21-22), and again, *"it shall not be so among you"* (Matt. 20:26KJV). Kingdom social culture is supposed to be evident in our daily activities and encounters.

KINGDOM COMPONENTS

All kingdoms are comprised of a number of components necessary for them to function effectively. All kingdoms, including the Kingdom of God, have:

- A Health program – healing;

- An Education program – Teaching ministry of the Holy Spirit;
- A Taxation system – Tithing;
- A central Communication system – Gifts of the Spirit;
- A Diplomatic Corps - Ambassadors of Christ;
- A System of Administration – the Ministration of the Spirit through mankind called the Church; and,
- An Economy – a system of Giving and Receiving (seed time and harvest time).

A careful study of the biblical message and the presentation of the message of the Kingdom of heaven by Jesus will illustrate the presence of all these components and characteristics of life in the Kingdom of God.

However, the most outstanding element distinguishing the Kingdom of God from every other kingdom is the concept that *all* of its citizens are relatives of the King, and are kings themselves. This was the message brought to earth by the Lord Jesus Christ.

A CONTRAST OF KINGDOMS

The buses lined the streets of the small town, bringing tourists from far and near to visit and photograph the little wooden house. Many traveled over seas to see this antique structure that had no architectural relationship to the modern concrete jungle that surrounded it. It looked like a slice of history served on the streets of the 21st century. It had now become the source of new tourist dollars for the staggering local economy and provided much needed jobs for the citizens of this small town.

However, it wasn't that long ago that this same old house was falling apart, dilapidated and an eyesore. Its walls held many memories and stories of the great past of the city. Some of the citizens demanded that it be taken down because it was affecting the real estate value of their properties. However, an old man who looked and acted almost as old as the little house began a petition to save the quaint little structure. Finally, he gained enough support to qualify the structure for the city conservation and preservation and antiquities act, and so began the long journey of restoration of this masterpiece of historical architecture.

Being a visitor to the city, I wanted to meet the old man and requested my driver take me to his house so I might hear the full story of the salvation of the condemned house.

A Lesson in Restoration

As the car pulled up to the fence surrounding the old wooden house with the paint peeling, three dogs ran out to meet us with unexpectedly friendly barks. The old man sitting in his creaky rocking chair beckoned to us as if he had been waiting for us for years. I stepped onto the porch and sat on an old crate he provided for us to rest. After I introduced myself, he asked what was our interest in the house. I asked him to tell me how he saved that house from impending destruction. With a twinkle in his eyes, he gathered his thoughts and proceeded to take me on a mental journey that held my attention like a child hearing a tale for the first time.

He spoke fondly of the history of this little old house and of his childhood experiences with its life. When I asked him about the restoration process, he told me a story I will never forget. He said that the house was a *genuine* restoration. "What do you mean by genuine restoration?" I asked. "Well," he replied, "You see, some so-called restorations are not genuine because they substitute materials for the original." Then gesturing toward the city square, he said, "But that project is genuine restoration because the architects went back to the archives and located the original drawings, then used the exact same materials for every part of the restoration reconstruction. In fact, the little house looks just like it did the day it was built."

"So true restoration requires the original plans and materials to be complete and genuine," I asked. "Absolutely! This is why the value of the restored house is worth more than the towering skyscrapers surrounding it," answered the old man. I left that porch that day with a greater appreciation for the complicated process called restoration and also understood more fully the great restoration program the Creator has been executing on this earth.

The divine strategy devised by the all-wise Creator follows the same principle as that of the old man's story. The loss of heaven's Kingdom on earth through Adam's disobedient act and, subsequently, the loss of its earthly envoy, the Holy Spirit, demanded restoration. This required a heavenly program for earth preservation. This program became known as the redemptive work of God. The goal of the program is the recovery and reestablishment of the Kingdom of heaven on earth and the reinstatement of mankind as its legal kingly representative.

The divine strategy was the return of the original Adam to earth to reconstruct the old Adam that had failed. The means would be the coming of the Messiah King to redeem, restore and reconnect man back to heaven's government once again. This promise of a royal seed in Genesis 3:15 established the coming of God in the flesh as a legal redeemer with all the rights to enter earth's realm to achieve this goal.

This declaration was known as "the promise" and activated the long historical expectation of a Messiah king destined to redeem all men and restore them back to their kingly position.

This process included the calling and appointment of a specific line through which this great king would come. Divine prerogative then chose an obedient man named Abraham (Genesis 12:1-4) to whom the promise was given of the coming of the Kingdom seed to redeem and restore, not just his nation, but all the nations of the world of mankind.

I will make you into a great nation and I will bless you; I will make your name great, and you will be a blessing. I will bless those who bless you, and whoever curses you I will curse; and all peoples on earth will be blessed through you" (Gen. 12:2-3).

MISUNDERSTANDING THE MESSAGE AND THE METHOD

The greatest danger in life is the misconstruing of a concept. A careful study of the promise will show that the promise was made "to" the nations "through" Abraham. This promise was the material for the introduction of prophets to the world. All the prophets of the Old Testament were raised up primarily to continually proclaim this promise of the coming messianic king, who would restore the Kingdom our father, Adam, lost.

Abraham had a son of promise as promised, Isaac, who had two sons named Jacob and Esau. Jacob was chosen by God to be the line for the seed of the messiah king and his name was changed by God Himself to Israel, which means "prince with God." Perhaps this was to confirm the royal line of descendants. Israel had 12 sons who became known as the 12 tribes or clans of Israel and collectively as the Israelites.

The Hebrews or Israelites were reminded of the promise from generation to generation, that the Messiah king would come and through Him all the nations of the earth would be blessed. However, they as a people misunderstood the promise and made themselves the object of the promise rather than the conduit. God had promised Abraham that the Messiah would come through his seed to redeem the world, but the Israelites used the choice of their line as a distinguishing factor to separate themselves from the very people they were to serve.

They developed a self-centered religion that condemned the world to which they were appointed to deliver the Redeemer, rather than God's intention of a Kingdom of heaven on earth. Israel became the masters of misinformation. This error has left scars throughout history and continues to feed the remnant of Judaism today. This is where the great religion of Judaism was born, causing the reactionary development of many other religions of today. Over the past 3,000 years, the message of the Kingdom was gradually buried in the graveyard of religion.

The Promise of Kingdom Rediscovery

The Old Testament is earth's file of heaven's record of the promise of the coming of the King and the Kingdom. All the prophecies were about His arrival and what He would bring; the laws given to Moses foreshadowed the laws and principles of the Kingdom. There are thousands of references to this specific announcement and a few are worth reviewing:

Moses predicted it:

The Lord your God will raise up for you a prophet like me from among your own brothers. You must listen to Him (Deut. 18:15).

David spoke of the Kingdom:

Your kingdom is an everlasting kingdom, and Your dominion endures through all generations (Ps. 145:13).

Isaiah saw the coming of the King and the Kingdom in detail:

For to us a child is born, to us a son is given, and the government will be on His shoulders. And He will be called Wonderful Counselor, Mighty God, Everlasting Father, Prince of Peace. Of the increase of His government and peace there will be no end. He will reign on David's throne and over his kingdom, establishing and upholding it with justice and righteousness from that time on and forever. The zeal of the Lord Almighty will accomplish this (Isa. 9:6-7).

Daniel saw the King and the Kingdom in graphic detail:

In my vision at night I looked, and there before me was one like a son of man, coming with the clouds of heaven. He approached the Ancient of Days and was led into His presence. He was given authority, glory and sovereign power; all peoples, nations and men of every language worshiped Him. His dominion is an everlasting dominion that will not pass away, and His kingdom is one that will never be destroyed (Dan. 7:13-14).

So he told me and gave me the interpretation of these things: "The four great beasts are four kingdoms that will rise from the earth. But the saints of the Most High will receive the kingdom and will possess it forever—yes, for ever and ever" (Dan. 7:16b-18).

As I watched, this horn was waging war against the saints and defeating them, until the Ancient of Days came and pronounced judgment in favor of the saints of the Most High, and the time came when they possessed the kingdom (Dan. 7:21-22).

But the court will sit, and his power will be taken away and completely destroyed forever. Then the sovereignty, power and greatness of the kingdoms under the whole heaven will be handed over to the saints, the people of the Most High. His kingdom will be an everlasting kingdom, and all rulers will worship and obey Him. This is the end of the matter. I, Daniel, was deeply troubled by my thoughts, and my face turned pale, but I kept the matter to myself (Dan. 7:26-28).

It is incredible to read these few scriptures and see, without a doubt, that the message of the Bible is about the coming of a kingdom, not a religion. However, the announcement of the Old Testament was about the coming of a prophet who would prepare the way and introduce the Messiah-King to the world personally. This was referring to John the Baptist. Let's read the prophecy from Malachi:

> Remember the law of my servant Moses, the decrees and laws I gave him at Horeb for all Israel. See, I will send you the prophet Elijah before that great and dreadful day of the Lord comes. He will turn the hearts of the fathers to their children, and the hearts of the children to their fathers; or else I will come and strike the land with a curse (Mal. 4:4-6).

So we see that the restoration plan of God was in motion from its earliest announcement to the adversary in Genesis, chapter 3. The prophecy stated that He would come and prepare the people for the entrance of the King and the Kingdom.

THE LONG WAIT—4,000 YEARS

According to biblical chronology, despite the possibility that the earth may have been in existence much longer, the creative act of God's making man is determined to be at least six thousand years ago. If we were to use this measure to calculate the length of God's redemptive drama for mankind, then the promise of the coming Messiah King would have occurred 4,000 years before the birth of John the Baptist. This means God waited for 4,000 years before He sent His Messiah King to earth. The question is why?

WAITING FOR A KINGDOM MODEL

God is a great communicator. He knew that He could not fully reveal the good news of His Kingdom until an environment existed in which people could understand the message. Only when the time was right could Christ come. Jesus could not come until a Kingdom model existed as a visual illustration to help people understand His teachings on the Kingdom. Only in the "fullness of time" could the Kingdom be revealed.

The same chapter of Genesis that describes the fall of man also announces God's promised solution, but many millennia would pass before its fulfillment. Because of the serpent's (satan's) role in tempting the first human couple to sin, God pronounced a curse on him, which also foretold his future doom: "So the Lord God said to the serpent, 'Because you have done this, cursed are you above all the livestock and all the wild animals! You will crawl on your belly and you will eat dust all the days of your life. And I will put enmity between you and the woman, and between your offspring and hers; He will crush your head, and you will strike His heel'" (Gen. 3:14-15). God promised that one of Eve's offspring ("seed" in the KJV) would crush the serpent's head, inflicting a fatal wound. That "seed" would be Jesus Christ.

When Jesus appeared preaching the Kingdom of heaven, He was the culmination of thousands of years of preparation in God's plan. What was God waiting for? Throughout history God was setting the stage and preparing an environment for His Son's appearance.

PREPARING FOR THE KING

Adam and Eve sinned by disobeying God and by this action they cut off themselves (as well as all future generations of human beings) from His Kingdom. The first significant biblical figure after Adam and Eve was Noah, a righteous man who believed in and followed God. He and his family survived the great flood by riding it out in an ark. Afterwards, however, Noah planted a vineyard and got drunk. Eventually his sons went their own ways and forgot God. Their descendants fell into idol worship and other kinds of evil. The time was not yet right for the Kingdom.

Ten generations after Noah, God spoke to Abram, a descendant of Noah's son Shem. God revealed Himself to Abraham and made a covenant with him that would make of him a great nation. From Abraham came Isaac, the son born to him in his old age. Still, God had no model of the Kingdom.

Isaac had two sons, Esau and Jacob. God appeared to Jacob and said, "I will make of you a great nation. Your name will now be Israel." Israel had 12 sons, who were the fathers of the 12 tribes of the nation of Israel. God was working toward His model. Through Moses, He delivered the Israelites from slavery in Egypt, brought them into the desert, and told them, "You will be My people and I will be your God. I will lead you into the land I promised your forefathers." In other words, He was saying, "I will be your King and you will be My Kingdom."

After awhile, however, the people of Israel got tired of a God they could not see and longed for a king they could see. God never desired for them to have an earthly king. This was not the appropriate model that He was seeking. Nevertheless, God gave in to their wishes and instructed the prophet Samuel to anoint Saul as king of Israel. Because the nation of Israel rejected God in favor of an earthly king, the time still was not right for the Kingdom of heaven to be revealed.

A Long Succession of Kings

After a promising start, Saul disobeyed God to the point at which God rejected him as king. God then chose David, a man after His own heart, to be king in Saul's place. David was a good king and a mighty warrior who loved God. He was also a poet and worshiper whose songs comprise the bulk of the longest book in the Bible: the Psalms. David was the first to informally combine the functions of priest and king. He worshiped and wrote worship songs, but he also administered government wisely and ably. A model of God's Kingdom was beginning to emerge.

Then David disappointed God by committing adultery with Bathsheba and compounding his sin by trying to cover it up. He arranged to have her husband, Uriah, killed. From then until the end of his life, trouble dogged David's steps. After the death of Solomon, David's wise and capable son and successor, the kingdom they had built split in two as ten tribes rebelled against the house of David. The time still was not right for the Kingdom of heaven to be revealed.

Following a long succession of kings, most of whom rejected God and served idols, first the northern kingdom of Israel and then the southern kingdom of Judah fell to outside conquerors. The northern kingdom was assimilated into the Assyrian empire and ceased to exist. The kingdom of Judah was conquered by the Babylonians, and the brightest and best of her people were carried into exile for 70 years.

Daniel, one of the exiles and an official in the Babylonian government, received a powerful vision from God that showed him that the

Kingdom was not dead and forgotten. God was still working toward His model, preparing for the "fullness of time" when His Son would come and reveal the Kingdom. Daniel spoke of a "son of man" who would do great things. Several hundred years later, Jesus would refer to Himself as the Son of man, His favorite self-designation.

Babylonians, Greeks, and Romans

The Babylonians fell to the Persians, who allowed the Jews to return to their homeland and rebuild their Temple and the city of Jerusalem. The Persians fell to the Greeks, whose great tradition of philosophy influenced the entire Mediterranean world. In time, the Greek Empire fell to the Romans, with their genius for military campaigns, law, and government administration. At last, the time for which God had been preparing drew near. The Roman Empire was the first in history with a structure and administration that resembled the Kingdom of God. Finally, God had His model.

Unlike the empires that preceded it, when Rome invaded and conquered a country, it set up its own administration with its own governor appointed by the emperor, but left the indigenous people in the land. Rome governed its conquered territory through appointed representatives who ruled with the authority of the emperor himself. The job of a Roman governor was to govern his province in such a way as to make it a reflection of Rome.

Rome became the greatest empire in history because it had a system of government that worked better than any that had gone before. It was a simple system, really: take over territory, leave the people in the land, but appoint a governor and establish an administration that will turn them into Romans.

Everything was now set. The Roman Empire provided the perfect model for the message of the Kingdom of God because it contained the concepts of the Kingdom that would make the message of Jesus easily understood. God's Kingdom model was in place. The time had come for God to send His Son. The time had come for the Kingdom of heaven to be revealed.

JUST AT THE RIGHT TIME

The Bible says that when the fullness of time came, God sent His Son, Jesus Christ, into the world (see Gal. 4:4). This means that God waited to send Jesus until the situation was ripe. Jesus came at just the right moment and place in history. What made this particular time 2,000 years ago right? Among other things, the time was right because there was a great earthly kingdom in place that could provide tangible, visible illustrations for Jesus' teachings about the Kingdom. The Roman Empire served as a model.

Under Caesar, the Roman Empire was a kingdom, not a democracy. Caesar was a king, not a president. During Jesus' day Rome ruled most of the known world. Its government, laws, institutions, and culture were everywhere. Every word that Jesus spoke about the Kingdom of God had a physical equivalent in Rome, making His message easier to understand for the people who listened to Him.

For example, the Roman senate was called the *ecclesia,* a Greek word that means "assembly," or "called-out ones." Greek and Latin were both widely spoken throughout the Empire. Jesus spoke Aramaic, the common language of the Jews of Palestine, but the Gospels were originally written in Greek. The Gospel writers use the word *ecclesia* in passages where Jesus talks about building His "Church." Just as Caesar had an assembly of called-out ones—the Senate—so also did Jesus Christ, the Son of the living God and King of kings have His assembly of called-out ones—His Church.

IMAGE OF A KING

Caesar issued coins stamped with his image and inscription. People understood that whatever bore Caesar's image belonged to Caesar and he had every right to claim it. Likewise, they could understand that whatever bore God's image and stamp of ownership belonged to God and was His for the claiming. When we come to Jesus and give Him our lives, the first thing He does is change our name. He gives us His name and calls us His sons and daughters. John tells us that to those who believe in His name He gives the right to become children of God (see John 1:12). As children of God, we are joined together with Christ and seated with Him on His throne in heaven next to our Father.

The Bible says that as believers we are citizens of heaven. That remains true no matter where we go. Whenever I travel internationally, I carry my passport with me, which identifies me as a Bahamian citizen to every foreign official who needs to see it. I do not have to be *in* the Bahamas to be a Bahamian; I am still a Bahamian citizen whether I am in the United States, Europe, or South America. Likewise, we do not have to be *in* heaven to be citizens there. Right now, we live on earth, but are citizens and ambassadors of the heavenly Kingdom, which is our true home.

You Are a King!

When Jesus stood before Pontius Pilate mere hours before His crucifixion, the Roman governor was surprised at His silence in the face of the accusations that had been brought against Him. At one point Pilate asked:

> *"Do You refuse to speak to me?...Don't You realize I have power either to free You or to crucify You?" Jesus answered, "You would have no power over Me if it were not given to you from above. Therefore the one who handed Me over to you is guilty of a greater sin"* (John 19:10-11).

As the Roman governor of Judea, Pilate represented the full power and authority of the Emperor himself. The full force of the mightiest empire in history backed Pilate's words, yet Jesus said that all that power had come from above, meaning, from His Father. This was Kingdom talk, and Jesus was saying that His Kingdom was greater than Rome's because it was from His Kingdom that Rome received its power.

At another point, Pilate questioned Jesus about His Kingdom:

> *"Are You the king of the Jews?" "Is that your own idea," Jesus asked, "or did others talk to you about Me?" "Am I a Jew?" Pilate replied. "It was Your people and Your chief priests who handed You over to me. What is it You have done?" Jesus said, "My kingdom is not of this world. If it were, My servants would fight to prevent My arrest by the Jews. But now My kingdom is from another place." "You are a king, then!" said Pilate. Jesus answered, "You are right in saying I am a king. In fact, for this reason I was born, and for this I came into*

the world, to testify to the truth. Everyone on the side of truth listens to Me." "What is truth?" Pilate asked (John 18:33b-38a).

Jesus answered Pilate plainly, acknowledging that He was both a King and that His Kingdom was "from another place," that is, not from the earth. His Kingdom is a kingdom of truth, for He came "to testify to the truth." All who desire the truth listen to Him. Therefore, Christ's Kingdom of truth is made up of citizens who are not only truth seekers but also truth followers. This alone makes His Kingdom unique, completely different from the kingdoms of the world.

As believers, we live on earth but our citizenship is in the Kingdom of heaven, and all the resources, authority, and power of that Kingdom are available to us as we seek to live as faithful and responsible ambassadors of our King. When someone asks us, "Where are you from?" we should give careful thought to our answer. The more we learn to think like Kingdom citizens, the more we will act like Kingdom citizens. The more we act like Kingdom citizens, the more we will proclaim the gospel of the Kingdom to a lost world, because that is our primary dominion mandate. It is important that we learn to live distinct Kingdom lives so that others can tell the difference between the kingdoms of this world and the Kingdom of God.

Every human being who has ever lived, has faced the same tension: being designed for one kingdom, yet forced to live in another. Most people are never able to clearly define the problem. For them, life always seems somewhat out of kilter, purposeless, and full of misery, as if something just doesn't quite fit. They are generally dissatisfied and discontented with life, but don't really know why.

Nothing works accurately when it is removed from the environment for which it was designed. A fish out of water will quickly suffocate; a human being under water without special breathing apparatus will soon drown.

GOD CREATED A WORLD JUST FOR YOU

One of the fundamental principles of creation is that whenever God creates something, He designs it according to its purpose and intended environment. In other words, when God created birds to fly, He gave them wings and the desire to fly. When God created fish to swim, He put in them the ability to swim and gave them gills so they could breathe in water. When God created mankind to have dominion over the earth, He imparted to us the ability to govern, rule, lead, and manage the earth, its creatures, and resources. We are designed to rule, not to be ruled. We are designed to govern, not to be governed. We are designed to manage, not to be managed. We are designed to lead, not to follow.

Whenever anyone tries to tell us what to do, even someone in a legitimate position of authority, there arises in us a spirit or attitude of resistance. It is our nature to resist being ruled or controlled by others. This is due in part to our sinful nature, which we inherited from Adam and Eve, and which the Bible says is always in rebellion against God, who is the ultimate and absolute authority. Adam and Eve sinned when, out of pride, they sought to be equal with God, their Creator, and free from His authority over them.

Our resistance to others ruling over us is also due to the spirit of leadership that God placed in us when He created us. God's purpose was for us to rule over the created order as vice-regents under His authority. He designed us for that purpose and put in us the appropriate spirit and innate ability to fulfill our destiny. Sin distorted and exaggerated that spirit, pushing it beyond the bounds that God intended. Our natural tendency is to resist *all* authority, including God's.

One reason so many of us experience frustration in life is because our environment has changed. We were designed to rule our lives and environment but instead we live in a world where we are ruled by our own pride, lust, passion, greed, and selfishness. We are dominated by the adversary, satan, the author of sin and the instigator of humanity's downfall. God designed us for mastery, yet that is not the reality we experience in our daily living. We are frustrated because we are not fulfilling our purpose. We do not function properly because we are not living in the environment for which we were designed.

The key to fulfilled and purposeful living is discovering how to regain our place of dominion, to return to our position of leadership in the earthly domain as God originally intended. To do this, we must understand the contrasts between the two kingdoms that envelop our lives as well as how we are to integrate ourselves properly into these two different worlds.

THE SEEDS OF LEADERSHIP

When God created us, He gave us everything we needed to fulfill His original plan and purpose. Because God designed us to lead, the seeds of leadership lie within us, dormant until they are ready to be activated by the power of God. For this reason, leadership is not something we should have to *study* as much as something that is already inside us. It is a matter of discovering and nurturing those powers of leadership within us.

Within the earthly realm, God has given us great freedom. Ultimately, the kind of leaders we become and the degree of dominion we exercise depends upon us. God will never violate our freedom or override the dominion spirit He placed within us. Although, I must say that He might make life awfully unbearable for us until we turn toward Him. The Holy Spirit will never force our hand. But as we allow Him, the Holy Spirit will convict us, guide us, and lead us, but He will never *drive* us.

Some of you may question this concept of the leadership potential within you. Maybe you consider yourself to be a follower and not a leader. Maybe you think you don't have the skills, qualities, ability, or experience to be a leader. Perhaps you have accepted the negative things others have said about you. In truth, it does not matter what other people say or think, or even what we think of ourselves. What matters is how God sees us, and He sees us as leaders and rulers in the earthly domain. He created us for this purpose and designed us with the necessary abilities to fulfill our destiny.

As Creator, God knows what is inside each one of us because He put it there. Whenever God speaks to you, He addresses you based on what He knows about you, not on what other people think they know.

CALLED TO DO THE IMPOSSIBLE

The Bible is full of stories of people who were called out of ordinary circumstances and challenged by God to do the impossible. When childless Abraham and Sarah were in their old age, far beyond the normal years for childbearing, God told them, "You will have a son, and he will grow into a great nation."

The Lord appeared to Gideon, the youngest of his family, which was of the least of the tribes of Israel, and He addressed him as "mighty warrior" (Judg. 6:12) and used him to deliver his people from the marauding Midianites.

In the eyes of his family, David may have been only a runt, useful for nothing but herding sheep. Nevertheless, God said, "You are a king," and sent Samuel to anoint him as such.

Seeing Joseph while he was a slave in Egypt, God said, "You are a ruler," and elevated him to the position of prime minister under Pharaoh.

When God speaks to us, He always speaks to the *real* person, not the person others see or even how we see ourselves. He looks beyond our external circumstances and personal characteristics as He addresses the leader inside us. No matter who we are, where we are, or what we do, God wants to deploy us into leadership. Wherever we work, whatever our career, we should think of our employment not as just a job but as an opportunity God has given us to release our leadership abilities. We should not complain about our wages or salary because we are already worth more than anyone could ever pay us. Work is not about simply making money in order to live. Work is also about being trained to assume our rightful place of leadership in the world.

As believers, we are all children of the King. The first step in successfully navigating between two kingdoms is learning how to think and act like the King's children. In spiritual reality we are all princes and princesses, but practically speaking most of us are not there yet because negative thinking has stunted our mental processes. Because we never learned to think like royalty, we still act like the prodigal son, seeking only the servant's share.

God wants us to open our eyes to see the wonders of who we truly are—His children—and reach out to claim all that is ours by right of sonship. It all comes down to a decision that each of us alone must make:

whether we will live as sons and daughters in the Kingdom of God, or as subjects in the kingdom of the world.

KINGDOMS IN CONFLICT

God reigns as King and absolute Sovereign over all things in both the spiritual and physical realms. After He created the earth with all its varied plant and animal life, He created mankind to rule over it. By His design we are rulers over the earthly domain. God is King of the universe, and we are His ruling representatives in the physical realm. The earth is our designated territory. As God's vice-regents in this world, *we are the Kingdom of God on earth.* The Kingdom of God, therefore, is not the earth itself, but the ones chosen to function as His rulers in the earthly domain. This planet is not the Kingdom of God. God's Kingdom is *us* carrying out His dominion on this planet. God's Kingdom is manifest in His people rather than in a particular place.

Psalm 115:16 says, *"The highest heavens belong to the Lord, but the earth He has given to man."* Every king or ruler must have territory to rule. Heaven is God's territory; the earth is ours. We were born to dominate earth, not heaven. That is why heaven is always a temporary excursion for the human spirit; it is not our territory.

Jesus spoke constantly about the Kingdom. Sometimes He referred to the "Kingdom of God," and other times to the "Kingdom of heaven." One deals with the person while the other deals with the place. Essentially, both phrases are the same, with one distinction. Whenever Jesus mentions the "Kingdom of God," He is referring to the actual rule of God in the spiritual realm. When He says, the "Kingdom of heaven," He is talking about its "headquarters" and the heavenly invasion upon the earth, or the transfer of power from the spiritual realm to the physical.

The prayer of the Lord illustrates this truth when He prays that the will of God be done in the earth regions as it is done in heaven's realm. The first speaks to God's actual rulership, while the second speaks of the source of that invading powerful Kingdom and its impact on the regions of the earth. As His representatives we are called to enforce the rule of heaven in the affairs of man.

The Kingdom of God on earth, therefore, is God's authority within the heart and spirit of man, and the Kingdom of heaven is when that authority impacts the human earthly environment through His designated representatives.

In other words, we who are the "Kingdom of God" on earth can, through the Holy Spirit, take our King with us everywhere we go and impact our environment by helping bring the "Kingdom of heaven" to that place. This is what Jesus meant when He said, "Repent, for the kingdom of heaven is near" (Matt. 4:17). He had arrived, bringing the Kingdom with Him and in Him. With His Spirit in us, we, too, carry His Kingdom with us wherever we go.

A Kingdom of Ignorance

God's orderly design was disrupted by the fall of man. By their disobedience, Adam and Eve abdicated their throne of earthly dominion, yielding it to satan, the architect and instigator of their fall. This ushered in a counterfeit kingdom that the Bible calls the "kingdom of darkness," which is in constant conflict with the Kingdom of God. When man chose to will something other than the will of God, he created a great disturbance in the force and initiated a time of great darkness.

Frequently throughout the Bible, the word *darkness* is used as a symbol of ignorance, while the word *light* represents knowledge. The *kingdom of darkness*, then, "is a domain where the king rules by ignorance—not *in* ignorance, but *by* ignorance." Satan rules his kingdom of darkness by keeping his "subjects" in ignorance of the true nature of their environment and of the existence of God's Kingdom. He fills their heads with lies and deception. Satan controls his subjects by keeping them "in the dark" regarding spiritual truth. He blinds their minds lest they understand the glorious good news of Jesus and the Kingdom of heaven.

The apostle Paul stated it this way: *"The god of this age has blinded the minds of unbelievers, so that they cannot see the light of the gospel of the glory of Christ, who is the image of God"* (2 Cor. 4:4).

In contrast to the darkness of ignorance, light symbolizes knowledge. The Kingdom of God is a Kingdom of light, the light of the knowledge of the Lord. Proverbs 1:7 says, "The fear of the Lord is the *beginning* of knowledge, but fools despise wisdom and discipline" [emphasis mine]. In this verse, the word *fools* refers to "people who are morally deficient." God's Kingdom of light brings the knowledge of grace, forgiveness, and salvation in Christ. In his letter to the believers in the city of Colosse, Paul wrote of God as *"...the Father, who has qualified you to share in the inheritance of the saints in the kingdom of light. For He has rescued us from the dominion of darkness and brought us into the kingdom of the Son He loves, in whom we have redemption, the forgiveness of sins"* (Col. 1:12-14).

Darkness and light—ignorance and knowledge—are opposites that exist in continual conflict with each other. We either walk in the darkness of ignorance or in the light of knowledge. The two cannot coexist.

CREATING A LIGHT IN THE DARK PLACES

I have made it clear that there are two kingdoms with which we must deal on a daily basis. One is a counterfeit kingdom of darkness controlled by a false prince who rules by the power of deception and enforced ignorance. The other is the true and legitimate Kingdom ruled by the King of kings and Lord of lords, who rules by the power of light, knowledge, and truth.

God's plan is to restore His original design to rule the visible earthly realm from the invisible heavenly realm. This plan is accomplished through human beings who properly exercise their dominion over the earth. In order for us to fulfill our destiny we must overthrow satan from the throne of the earthly domain he seized illegitimately. From a spiritual standpoint, this has already happened through the death and resurrection of Jesus Christ: *"The reason the Son of God appeared was to destroy the devil's work"* (1 John 3:8b).

Jesus' death on the cross broke sin's power forever; His resurrection from the grave conquered death for all time: *"Where, O death, is your victory? Where, O death, is your sting?' The sting of death is sin, and the power of sin is the law. But thanks be to God! He gives us the victory through our Lord Jesus Christ"* (1 Cor. 15:55-57).

In a practical sense, from the beachhead established at Calvary, we must move forth in an all-out attack to free mankind from bondage to the devil and his evil kingdom of darkness. We who are in Christ must work to eliminate the ignorance of those still trapped in the darkness of satan's deceptions. The antidote to ignorance is knowledge. Knowledge comes through truth, and truth brings liberation. Jesus said, *"If you hold to My teaching, you are really My disciples. Then you will know the truth, and the truth will set you free....I tell you the truth, everyone who sins is a slave to sin. Now a slave has no permanent place in the family, but a son belongs to it forever. So if the Son sets you free, you will be free indeed"* (John 8:31-32; 34-36).

KNOWLEDGE: INFORMATION FROM GOD

Knowledge lies at the heart of the struggle between the two kingdoms, because knowledge is where the adversary mounted his original attack on humanity. Satan's most powerful weapon is ignorance, but to use it he must first destroy or distort true knowledge. That is exactly what he did with Adam and Eve in the Garden of Eden. He deceived and overcame them by attacking the source and substance of their knowledge.

The first thing God gave Adam for their protection was information: "You are free to eat from any tree in the garden; but you must not eat from the tree of the knowledge of good and evil, for when you eat of it you will surely die" (Gen. 2:16-17). Adam received knowledge; he *knew* what the boundaries were and what was expected of him. Furthermore, he passed this knowledge on to Eve after she appeared on the scene. As long as they obeyed God and respected His boundaries, they would live and prosper and enjoy unlimited fellowship with their Creator.

Satan, that serpent and deceiver, was very subtle in his approach. He did not launch a direct attack on God, but sowed seeds of distrust in Adam and Eve's minds that led them to doubt and question the truth and veracity of the knowledge God had given them and, therefore, to doubt God Himself.

Now the serpent was more crafty than any of the wild animals the Lord God had made. He said to the woman, "Did God really say, 'You must not eat from any tree in the garden'?" The woman said to the serpent, "We may eat fruit from the trees in the garden, but God did say, 'You must not eat fruit from the tree that is in the middle of the garden, and you must not touch it, or you will die.'" "You will not surely die," the serpent said to the woman. "For God knows that when you eat of it your eyes will be opened, and you will be like God, knowing good and evil" (Gen. 3:1-5).

Did God really say that?

The first thing the devil did was attempt to get Eve to doubt whether she correctly understood God's instructions: "Did God *really* say, 'You must not eat from any tree in the garden'?" Next, he suggested to her that God was not being straightforward with them in His prohibition against eating the fruit from the tree in the middle of the Garden. "You will not surely die…For God knows that when you eat of it your eyes will be opened, and you will be like God, knowing good and evil." In this he represented God as *knowing* both good *and* evil. In His omniscience, God understands the nature of evil, but in His *perfection* He does not *know* evil *experientially*. Satan knows evil because he is evil and, after their disobedience, Adam and Eve knew it also.

As a result of satan's ploy, Adam and Eve developed a distorted understanding of the knowledge God had given them. They succumbed to the devil's manipulation and trickery to become "like God," although *they were already like Him*. Once they took the devil's bait, they fell into sin and became like the devil. In their sin, Adam and Eve, rather than becoming like God, became less like God than they were before.

BATTLE OF THE KINGDOMS

Satan's tactics have not changed much. Today he still attacks us most often by attempting to draw us into doubting the knowledge we have received from the Lord. God tells us one thing; satan tells us another. For example, God might say, "By My Son's stripes 2,000 years ago, you are healed today." Satan says, "You still feel the pain." Two conflicting pieces of information come into our minds, and we must decide which one is real, which one is true, which one we will believe and stand upon, and which one we will reject or disregard. If we choose to believe in the pain, then we remain "in the dark" concerning our healing.

This is an example of how the two kingdoms work against each other. The kingdom of darkness is out to deceive and destroy us. God's Kingdom of light gives us life because Jesus Christ, to whom the Kingdom belongs, is both light and life. As John the apostle wrote concerning

Jesus, *"In Him was life, and that life was the light of men"* (John 1:4). God's plan, which will surely come to pass at the time of His choosing, is for the Kingdom of His Son to undermine and replace the adversary's kingdom of darkness. On that day will come true the words of Revelation 11:15: *"The kingdom of the world has become the kingdom of our Lord and of His Christ, and He will reign for ever and ever."*

Until that day, we who are believers must navigate the delicate balance of living in the kingdom of darkness, while walking in the Kingdom of light. The Lord has called us to "walk in the light as He is in the light" (1 John 1:7). Jesus said, *"You are the light of the world....let your light shine before men, that they may see your good deeds and praise your Father in heaven"* (Matt. 5:14,16).

KNOWLEDGE IS IMPORTANT

The kingdom of darkness gets its power from that which we do not know. The truth we are ignorant of cannot protect us against satan's deception. That is why we must devote ourselves to studying, learning, experiencing, and practicing the Word of God. The light of knowledge dispels the darkness of deception and ignorance; the light of truth destroys the darkness of lies and error.

Satan hates the Word of God. He has no weapon that can stand against it. Whenever God's Word is taught or proclaimed, satan immediately attempts to steal it away or to blind and confuse people's minds so that they do not understand and believe. As ruler of the kingdom of darkness, satan fears the light. He fears the One who is the light, and he fears all who walk in the light. Satan is afraid of us because, as believers, we are children of the light. We possess and display in our lives the divine light of truth and knowledge spelling his destruction.

It is important to know the difference between what the world calls knowledge and the true knowledge of the Kingdom of God. The Bible teaches that all of us, as descendants of Adam and Eve and spiritual heirs to their sinfulness, are born as children of darkness. This means that we are born in ignorance. Even as we grow, and no matter how much education we receive, our fundamental ignorance remains until it is removed in Christ. No matter how smart we are and no matter how many degrees or titles we may carry after our name, until we come to know God through faith in Christ and begin to obey His Word, we remain in the darkness of spiritual ignorance. Without spiritual enlightenment of the divine truth of Christ, all other knowledge ultimately is irrelevant.

Knowledge unenlightened by the truth of God is dark knowledge. We may have a B.S., an M.S., and a Ph.D., but without the Lord all we have is dark information. It may be sufficient to help us navigate in the world of darkness, but by itself will never lead us to the truth. Apart from the revelation of the Spirit of God, none of us could ever find our way into the light. Darkly educated people are like those whom Paul described to his young protégé, Timothy, as "always learning but never able to acknowledge the truth" (2 Tim. 3:7).

Darkness is the absence of accurate information about God. It is possible to spend a lifetime in the schools of the kingdom of darkness and never see the light. That is why Jesus told Nicodemus, an expert on the Jewish law, that he needed to be born again (see John 3:3). In effect, Jesus said to him, "Nicodemus, you need to start over. What you have learned up to now is no good." A person of great learning who does not know the Lord is nothing more than a highly educated fool.

SURRENDERING YOUR HEAVENLY PASSPORT

Whenever a citizen of a country is convicted of a crime against the state and is about to be incarcerated, one of the first things the government requires is that he surrender his passport. A passport is one of our most significant symbols of citizenship because it is an official document that identifies our legal status as a citizen of a specific nation. It grants us the freedom as citizens to travel outside our country and still enjoy all the rights and privileges that we have at home.

In requiring a citizen to surrender his passport, the government is saying, "You are under judgment and during that time have forfeited your citizenship rights." Citizens have the right to move freely, earn a living, own property, buy food, drive on the streets, pay taxes, and receive the benefits and services provided by their government. A citizen who is convicted of a crime has fallen out of favor or position with the government. During the terms of the sentence he must forgo many of those rights and privileges, particularly freedom of movement. Incarcerated prisoners must endure great restrictions of their personal freedom. The correctional system owns them and controls every aspect of their lives from the time they get up in the morning, to when they eat, what they do during the day, and when they go to bed.

This was Adam's experience when he disobeyed God's government. When Adam sinned, he lost his favored status. In other words, Adam fell out of position with the government and had all of his citizen rights cancelled. God took away his "passport" and Adam became a prisoner of darkness, a slave to sin, and was ruled by a "warden" named satan.

PRISONERS IN A FOREIGN LAND

Every human being has been held captive in this precarious predicament. This is the universal human dilemma: Until we are enlightened and set free by Christ, we are all prisoners in the kingdom of darkness. All of us are born in a prison of sin and darkness. Because of our sinful nature inherited from Adam, we are unrighteous. Being *unrighteous* means that while we are still created "in God's image" (although somewhat marred), "we have no Kingdom rights." Our citizenship is nonexistent until our unrighteous condition is removed.

In Luke 4:18-19 Jesus describes His purpose in coming to earth: *"The Spirit of the Lord is on Me, because He has anointed Me to preach good news to the poor. He has sent Me to proclaim freedom for the prisoners and recovery of sight for the blind, to release the oppressed, to proclaim the year of the Lord's favor."* Jesus came to restore our position in God's government—to make us righteous. He came to restore our "passport" so that we can once again claim and enjoy our citizen promises.

Until the right time for the coming of Jesus, God has set up a temporary government on earth called the covenant. The history, development, and specific circumstances of this covenant are related in the Old Testament. God established His covenant with Abram (later called Abraham), and promised to make of him a great nation through which all the people of the earth would be blessed (see Gen. 12:2-3). Even though Abraham and his wife Sarai (later called Sarah) were childless and far beyond childbearing age, God assured them that this great nation of people would descend from a son born to them in their old age (see Gen. 15:4). The Scripture says that in light of this promise, "Abram believed the Lord, and He credited it to him as righteousness" (Gen. 15:6).

Righteousness means being in right position with God, getting into relationship with God's government and able to claim all the benefits promised in the covenant. When Abram believed God, the Lord declared him righteous on the basis of his faith, and Abram became a qualified citizen of the Kingdom of God. Abram received his "passport."

THE COMING OF THE GOD-MAN

Centuries later, Jesus would appear. In order to resolve the predicament, God would visit planet earth in the person of His Son. As a descendant of Adam He would open the way for man to become righteous. This would be accomplished through the offering of His blood on the cross. Jesus came to bring us back and synchronize our lives with the government of God, so that we can once more claim our citizen rights. It is in this manner that God sought to reconcile us to Himself: "God made Him who had no sin to be sin for us, so that in Him we might become the righteousness of God" (2 Cor. 5:21).

The word *righteous* is a legal term, not a religious term, and means "to position oneself rightly." Jesus came to make us righteous again, to put us back in right relationship with God so that we are qualified to receive the promises of God. Understanding this is critical to developing solid Kingdom thinking. When we are in right relationship with God, He can extend His Kingdom—His rulership—into our lives, and rule the earth through us. It is as we rule the earth in the power and presence of God that the Kingdom of heaven impacts our planet through our physical lives.

A FULL PARDON FOR MANKIND

Through Christ, our sins are forgiven and we receive a full pardon from God. A pardon is a powerful and potentially dangerous thing because it is irreversible. Once a king or ruler has pardoned someone, that person is forever free and exonerated of the crime or offense for which they were previously under judgment. Unlike a parole, which is a probationary state that still carries restrictions for the parolee, a pardon cleans the slate completely. A pardon declares its recipient to be as innocent as if the offense never occurred. Once a person is pardoned, the government returns his or her passport, and from that moment forward that person is free to travel, work, engage in business, buy and sell, and enjoy all other citizen rights and privileges without limitation. A pardon justifies and reestablishes a person's righteousness in the eyes of the law.

That is what Jesus did for all of us on the cross. His death and shed blood bought our pardon and made us righteous in the eyes of God once more. Our Kingdom citizenship and rights were restored, and we were positioned once again as recipients and heirs of all God's promises.

Righteousness is made possible through Christ's death and resurrection, but it is imparted to us through faith, just as it was for Abraham. When we believe, we become children of God. As Paul wrote to the Galatian believers, "You are all sons of God through faith in Christ Jesus, for all of you who were baptized into Christ have clothed yourselves with Christ....If you belong to Christ, then you are Abraham's seed, and heirs according to the promise" (Gal. 3:26-27, 29).

Many centuries—millennia even—passed between the time Adam and Eve sinned in the Garden of Eden and the time Christ came to restore our righteousness and return our "passport" to God's Kingdom. If Christ's death on the cross was so critical to mankind's restoration, why did God wait so long to send Him to the earth?

PRINCIPLES

1. God's purpose was for us to rule over the created order as vice-regents under His authority.

2. Because God designed us to lead, the seeds of leadership lie within us, dormant until activated.

3. As God's vice-regents in this world, *we are the Kingdom of God on earth.*

4. The Kingdom of God on earth is God's rulership within the hearts and spirits of believers, and the Kingdom of heaven is when that rulership impacts the human earthly environment.

5. The Kingdom of God is a Kingdom of light, the light of the knowledge of the Lord.

6. The antidote to ignorance is knowledge. Knowledge comes through truth, and truth brings liberation.

7. Without spiritual enlightenment into the divine truth of Christ, all other knowledge ultimately means nothing.

8. Jesus came to restore our position in God's government—to make us righteous.

9. When we are in right relationship with God, He can extend His Kingdom—His rulership—into our lives, and rule the earth through us.

10. Through Christ, our sins are forgiven and we receive a full pardon from God.

11. Jesus could not come until a Kingdom model existed as a visual illustration to help people understand His teachings on the Kingdom.

12. Christ's Kingdom of truth is made up of citizens who are not only truth seekers but also truth followers.

"You can not lose what
you never had."

CHAPTER THREE

ENTER THE KING AND THE KINGDOM

THE BIRTH OF THE KINGDOM ANNOUNCER

A few years ago, just after September 11th, I was scheduled to speak at a conference in Pennsylvania. When I arrived at the Pittsburgh airport, I found an unusually large crowd clogging the terminal. After being detained for over an hour, our driver was finally allowed to go and get the car. I noticed as we emerged from the baggage claim area that it looked like a war zone. There were police, security and army officers everywhere. For a moment I thought some terrorist act had occurred. My driver worked up the nerve to ask one of the Army officers the reason for so much security activity. His answer shocked me. After warning us that traffic throughout the whole city would be heavy, he said we should be prepared to have our vehicle searched anytime, anywhere that day. The reason, he explained, for the heightened security was that the President of the United States was coming to Pittsburgh in three days. I could not believe what I was hearing. All of this commotion for a man who was not even in town yet, who was not arriving for three days! I asked the officer why all this activity so far in advance. "We are preparing for the coming of the President."

As we drove away I couldn't help but think that this is the very thing that occurs in all kingdoms when royalty is expected. In the Bahamas, where I was born and still live, when we were a colony of the United Kingdom of Great Britain, whenever the Queen or any member of the royal family were scheduled to visit our island territory, preparations began months in advance. The streets were swept, streetlights cleaned, schools painted, flags hung and so much more—the principle being, whenever a sovereign is to arrive, it is announced and preparations are made far in advance. Even the people have to be prepared.

This was the role of John the Baptist, the announcer of the King. John was keeping Kingdom royal protocol. His job was to prepare the people, the nation and the way for the coming of the King who would bring the Kingdom. The scripture describes John in this way,

In those days John the Baptist came, preaching in the Desert of Judea and saying, "Repent, for the kingdom of heaven is near." This is he who was spoken of through the prophet Isaiah: "A voice of one calling in the desert, 'Prepare the way for the Lord, make straight paths for Him'" (Matt. 3:1-3).

John replied in the words of Isaiah the prophet, "I am the voice of one calling in the desert, 'Make straight the way for the Lord'" (John 1:23).

Please note that John's message was not about a religion, but the Kingdom of heaven. It is important to understand that John was the most unique prophet of the entire Bible. In fact, Jesus stated that John was the greatest of all the prophets that had ever lived.

I tell you the truth: Among those born of women there has not risen anyone greater than John the Baptist; yet he who is least in the kingdom of heaven is greater than he (Matt. 11:11).

Why does John hold such a prominent position among the prophets? Because all the prophets before John spoke only of the coming of the Messiah King and the coming of the Kingdom, while John had the privilege of announcing, presenting, meeting and baptizing the King of the Kingdom.

UNDERSTANDING OUR ROLE AS KINGS

The birth of Jesus was announced as the birth of a king, not a priest. This is very important because it emphasizes the primary focus of the mission of Jesus and His purpose for coming to earth. Hear His words concerning His purpose for coming. His priesthood was His redemptive function, but to be king was His eternal disposition.

"You are a king, then!" said Pilate.

Jesus answered, "You are right in saying I am a king. In fact, for this reason I was born, and for this I came into the world, to testify to the truth. Everyone on the side of truth listens to Me" (John 18:37).

From then on, Pilate tried to set Jesus free, but the Jews kept shouting, "If you let this man go, you are no friend of Caesar. Anyone who claims to be a king opposes Caesar" (John 19:12).

But He said, "I must preach the good news of the kingdom of God to the other towns also, because that is why I was sent" (Luke 4:43).

WHAT WAS THE MISSION AND PURPOSE OF JESUS?

The greatest tragedy in life is not death: It is life without a purpose. The most important discovery in life is the discovery of purpose. Purpose is defined as the original intent or motivation for something. Purpose is also defined as the reason or desired result for the initiation or an action of production of a thing. Simply put, purpose is the "why" of a thing. Without a clear understanding of purpose, life becomes an experiment. Where purpose is not known, abuse is inevitable. Without purpose, activity has no meaning and time and energy are misused. Purpose determines what is right. Purpose protects us from doing something good at the expense of the right. Purpose is the predetermined, established, intended result of a thing.

The great king of Israel, Solomon, expressed the critical importance of the concept of purpose in his Book of Proverbs this way,

Many are the plans in a man's heart, but it is the Lord's purpose that prevails (Prov. 19:21).

This statement implies the priority of purpose as compared to a plan of action. It suggests that the most important interest of the Creator is His original intent for His actions and creation.

This is why we must seriously and carefully consider, when discussing the most important subject of God's purpose and plan for humanity, that we revisit the purpose, message, and assignment of Jesus Christ.

THE ORIGINAL MISSION OF JESUS

The controversial movie of 2004, *The Passion*, produced by actor/producer Mel Gibson, stirred the whole world about the life and death of Jesus Christ. There has been much controversy and debate down through the years over the life, message, death, and resurrection of Jesus Christ, especially within the religious community. There are many views and opinions as to what His real mission was. Scholars have dissected, examined, reviewed, revised and written volumes on these subjects. Yet many are still confused as to what His mission, message, methods, and purpose were for coming to earth.

However, for us to discover the original purpose and mission of Jesus, it should be obvious that we must consider His own declarations concerning His purpose and assignment for coming into the world. Let's read a few of them from the records of His close friends in the gospel narrative.

His first public statement was made at the beginning of His earthly mission, when He was 30 years old, after being baptized by His cousin John the Baptist, and completing 40 days of fasting, during which He overcame satan's temptations to compromise His assignment:

From that time on Jesus began to preach, "Repent, for the kingdom of heaven is near" (Matt. 4:17).

The word *near*, in some translations rendered "at hand," simply means "has arrived." In other words, His first declaration was the introduction and arrival of a kingdom, not a religion. In essence, He brought a government to earth. Let's look at some other declarations by Jesus concerning His purpose and mission on earth.

As you go, preach this message: "The kingdom of heaven is near" (Matt. 10:7).

But if I drive out demons by the Spirit of God, then the kingdom of God has come upon you (Matt. 12:28).

Therefore, the kingdom of heaven is like a king who wanted to settle accounts with his servants (Matt. 18:23).

And this gospel of the kingdom will be preached in the whole world as a testimony to all nations, and then the end will come (Matt. 24:14).

But He said, "I must preach the good news of the kingdom of God to the other towns also, because that is why I was sent." And He kept on preaching in the synagogues of Judea (Luke 4:43-44).

After this, Jesus traveled about from one town and village to another, proclaiming the good news of the kingdom of God (Luke 8:1a).

But the crowds learned about it and followed Him. He welcomed them and spoke to them about the kingdom of God, and healed those who needed healing (Luke 9:11).

But seek His kingdom, and these things will be given to you as well (Luke 12:31).

Do not be afraid, little flock, for your Father has been pleased to give you the kingdom (Luke 12:32).

The Law and the Prophets were proclaimed until John. Since that time, the good news of the kingdom of God is being preached, and everyone is forcing his way into it. It is easier for heaven and earth to disappear than for the least stroke of a pen to drop out of the Law (Luke 16:16-17).

I tell you the truth, anyone who will not receive the kingdom of God like a little child will never enter it (Luke 18:17).

And I confer on you a kingdom, just as My Father conferred one on Me (Luke 22:29).

Jesus said, "My kingdom is not of this world. If it were, My servants would fight to prevent My arrest by the Jews. But now My kingdom is from another place." "You are a king, then!" said Pilate. Jesus answered, "You are right in saying I am a king. In fact, for this reason I was born, and for this I came into the world, to testify to the truth. Everyone on the side of truth listens to Me" (John 18:36-37).

These are only a few of the declarations made by Jesus concerning His mission, purpose, and message and it is obvious that His intent was to declare, establish, and invite all men to enter the Kingdom of God.

This is in direct contrast with the focus on religious activity and religion's preoccupation with going to heaven. It seems as if the message and priority of Jesus was the occupation and reclamation of earth, rather than designing an escape hatch to heaven for mankind. There is a verse of scripture that has challenged my thinking for years and perhaps it may shed some light on this issue for you also.

Blessed are the meek, for they will inherit the earth (Matt. 5:5).

It is interesting to note that the promise is for the inheritance of earth rather than heaven. Also His dominion of earth and its environment was declared by Jesus as the return of the Kingdom of God to earth.

But if I drive out demons by the Spirit of God, then the kingdom of God has come upon you (Matt. 12:28).

This verse seems to indicate the return of the dominion power that Adam lost in his disobedience. Jesus came to earth, not to bring a religion, but a Kingdom—the governing influence of the Kingdom of heaven on earth. The message proclaims the opportunity for all mankind to regain its lost dominion over earth and its environment through the reception of the Holy Spirit of God and, consequently, the reconnection of earth with heaven. This is why it is called "good news" or gospel.

The message of the Kingdom of God is the most important news ever delivered to the human race. Jesus came to earth to announce the arrival of this Kingdom and to establish it in people's hearts through His death and resurrection. As the Son of God, Jesus Christ was the exact likeness of His Father and represented Him perfectly on earth. To all those who believed in and followed Him, Jesus restored their citizenship rights in the Kingdom of heaven and imparted His Spirit, so that they could represent Him and the government of heaven on earth. This representation is known as government diplomacy. The following statement is a political statement that is very common to all kingdoms, including our contemporary governments.

And I confer on you a kingdom, just as my Father conferred one on Me (Luke 22:29).

This statement is always used at the appointment of an official representative of a government to other nations. This is the position of an ambassador. This is not a religious designation, but a governmental one.

HEAVEN'S AMBASSADORS ON EARTH

Every nation appoints ambassadors and envoys to represent its interests to other nations. The Kingdom of heaven is no different, as it is the prototype of kingdoms. God chose to communicate the message of His Kingdom throughout the earth: not through *religious* people, but through *personal representatives*. God's chosen strategy for proclaiming His Kingdom was to employ *ambassadors*. An ambassador is a political appointee whose job is to represent and speak for his or her home government before the rulers of other countries. In the eyes of those rulers, the word of an ambassador *is* the word of the government that he or she represents. Good ambassadors never speak their personal opinions, but only the official policies of the government that appointed them.

In the same way, the people of God are His ambassadors on the earth. Scripture clearly teaches this. God chose Moses to deliver the Israelites from slavery in Egypt and then to represent Himself before them. Prophets represented God and spoke His messages of warning and judgment to a nation that had turned away from Him. In Second Corinthians 5:20, Paul writes, *"We are therefore Christ's ambassadors, as though God were making His appeal through us. We implore you on Christ's behalf: Be reconciled to God."* As ambassadors of heaven, we represent our Father's Kingdom on earth. If we are to be effective, it is important that we understand what we are talking about.

CHARACTERISTICS OF AN AMBASSADOR

An ambassador is a unique political creature in all kingdoms and his disposition must be understood fully, in order to appreciate the power and distinction of this revered position. Here are some very paramount qualities of an ambassador:

- Appointed by the king, not voted into position;
- Appointed to represent the state or kingdom;
- Committed only to the state's interests;
- Embodies the nation-state or kingdom;
- Totally covered by the state;
- Is the responsibility of the state;
- Totally protected by his government;
- Never becomes a citizen of the state or kingdom to which he is assigned;
- Can only be recalled by the king or president;
- Has access to all his nation's wealth for assignment;
- Never speaks his personal position on any issue, only his nation's official position; and,
- His goal is to influence the territory for his kingdom government.

All of these qualities and characteristics are embedded in the message and ministry of the Kingdom of God and are perfectly exemplified by our Chief Ambassador (Secretary of State) Jesus Christ.

All of these also apply to each citizen of the Kingdom of heaven who has been appointed by the government of heaven to represent heaven on earth. This is why Jesus admonished us to not worry about anything concerning our lives, but to focus on the Kingdom; then everything we need for life and fulfilling our Kingdom assignment on earth will be provided by the government of heaven.

Here are some ambassadorial statements and references expressed by the King, Jesus Himself, regarding His diplomatic duties in representing His heavenly government. These He transferred to you, who have submitted as citizens of the Kingdom of heaven.

Jesus said to them, "My Father is always at His work to this very day, and I, too, am working" (John 5:17).

Jesus gave them this answer: "I tell you the truth, the Son can do nothing by Himself; He can do only what He sees His Father doing, because whatever the Father does the Son also does (John 5:19).

By Myself I can do nothing; I judge only as I hear, and My judgment is just, for I seek not to please Myself but Him who sent Me (John 5:30).

Just as the living Father sent Me and I live because of the Father, so the one who feeds on Me will live because of Me (John 6:57).

I have much to say in judgment of you. But He who sent Me is reliable, and what I have heard from Him I tell the world. (John 8:26).

So Jesus said, "When you have lifted up the Son of Man, then you will know that I am the one I claim to be and that I do nothing on My own but speak just what the Father has taught Me. The one who sent Me is with Me; He has not left Me alone, for I always do what pleases Him" (John 8:28-29).

Do not believe Me unless I do what My Father does. (John 10:37).

For I did not speak of My own accord, but the Father who sent Me commanded Me what to say and how to say it. I know that His command leads to eternal life. So whatever I say is just what the Father has told Me to say (John 12:49-50).

Anyone who has seen Me has seen the Father. How can you say, "Show us the Father"? Don't you believe that I am in the Father, and that the Father is in Me? The words I say to you are not just My own. Rather, it is the Father, living in Me, who is doing His work. Believe me when I say that I am in the Father and the Father is in Me; or at least believe on the evidence of the miracles themselves. I tell you the truth, anyone who has faith in Me will do what I have been doing. He will do even greater things than these, because I am going to the Father (John 14:9-12).

Again Jesus said, "Peace be with you! As the Father has sent Me, I am sending you." And with that He breathed on them and said, "Receive the Holy Spirit" (John 20:21-22).

I declare that we are also ambassadors of our heavenly government, representing our government's mind, will, purposes and intent to the earth, so that His Kingdom can come and His will be done on earth just as it is in heaven. We are charged only to speak what our government speaks, not our own personal opinion or views. Therefore, whenever an ambassador is asked to comment on any issue, he is obligated to speak his government's position. He simply quotes the constitutional (the Bible) position on all matters. Go and be an ambassador of the government of heaven, not of a religion. Study your constitution to know and understand your government's position on all issues pertaining to life.

THE KINGDOM AND THE REPUBLIC

Most of us who are raised in a democratic society have trouble understanding the concept of a kingdom. For the same reason we also frequently have difficulty understanding the Bible, because the Bible is not about democracy. Since we live under a democratic system of government, we tend to assume that God is democratic. This is not so. Although many of the foundation stones of democracy are biblical, such as the principles of individual human rights, liberty, and dignity, democracy itself is not a biblical concept. Democracy arose in ancient Greece, a product of the thought of Greek philosophers like Plato, Socrates, and Aristotle. *Democracy is an invention of man*; it did not come from the Bible.

In our modern world, democracies usually take one of two forms: a republic or a parliamentary democracy. A republic is a democratic nation headed by a president elected by the people. Ultimate power in a republic lies with the citizens rather than with the leadership. The United States, Canada, Nigeria, England, Spain, Jamaica, Brazil or any other democratic form of government, or a parliamentary democracy like the Bahamas, are all republics because they have elected presidents.

I am a citizen of the Bahamas, which is a parliamentary democracy under a commonwealth of nations. The highest leadership position in our country is not an elected president, but an appointed governor, under whom is a prime minister elected by the people. The prime minister is the chief executive of the Bahamas and responsible for executing the mandates of the governor. After every election, the prime minister gives his governing plan to the governor who reviews and returns it. In a parliamentary democracy, the prime minister, although he is the chief executive, takes his orders from the governor, who holds the highest position. Symbolically, however, even the governor is not the ultimate authority because the Queen of England is, in name, the ruler of our country, even though she does not really govern anything. In our commonwealth of nations, she is the titular head of state.

Whether we live in a republic like the United States or in a parliamentary nation like the Bahamas, the problem we face as citizens of a democracy is understanding what it means as believers to live in a Kingdom. This is a very important distinction. The Bible teaches about a Kingdom ruled by God. A kingdom is diametrically opposed to a democracy. Living successfully in the Kingdom of God will require of us a complete mental reversal. We cannot be effective citizens of the Kingdom of God and continue to think democratically.

DEVELOPING A KINGDOM THINKING

The first recorded words of Jesus' public ministry directly address our need to shift our thinking and acting into a Kingdom context. Jesus, after being baptized by John in the Jordan River and spending 40 days in the wilderness being tempted by satan, embarked on His earthly mission:

From that time on Jesus began to preach, "Repent, for the kingdom of heaven is near" (Matt. 4:17).

Jesus came into the world to introduce God's plan for this planet, and the first thing He said was, "Repent!" In His very first statement to the world, Jesus began by telling us that we need to change our minds. That is essentially what the word *repent* means. Perhaps a better way of saying it is that we need to change our thinking or our mindset.

Literally speaking, to repent means to stop, turn around, and go in the opposite direction. It is like walking down a road, realizing you are headed in the wrong direction, and turning around 180 degrees to head in the right direction. This suggests action, but action follows thinking. Before we can turn around, we have to *decide* to turn around.

Some might even find Jesus' first word to us insulting, because He is saying, "You've got wrong thinking. Everything you've learned is wrong, and you need to change." For example, in our democratic environment we have been taught that governments operate by the will and vote of the people, even in choosing our own leader. In a democracy, every vote counts and every opinion is important. The majority rules. Not so in a kingdom. The vote of the people means nothing in a kingdom, and only one opinion matters—the king's.

There is no vote in the Kingdom of God; His Word is supreme and absolute. We do not vote for our Leader; He is already in place and His is a permanent office. God's tenure as King is eternal, a reign that will never end, neither by death nor by conquest. In God's Kingdom, our opinion is of no importance. His opinion is all that matters; His will and His ways supersede all others. Majority does not apply in the Kingdom of God. Even though a majority of the earth's population lives in ignorance of and rebellion toward God, He is and will remain the sovereign King of creation. *There is no vote in the Kingdom of God; His Word is supreme and absolute.*

CONTRASTING A KINGDOM WITH A DEMOCRACY

A kingdom and a democracy are two totally different worlds. That is why it is difficult for believers who were born in a democracy to live a strong Kingdom life. We want to debate the issues or interject our own thoughts and opinions. We try to reach consensus or compromise to keep everyone happy instead of simply recognizing that the King's Word is law. If God says that adultery is a sin, that is the word of the King, and His Word is the law. The matter is not open for discussion. We can debate God's words and decrees until we are blue in the face, but in the end all we will have to show for it are blue faces; His Word will still be the law. No matter what humanistic philosophy preaches from its pulpits in the schools and in our courts, God's law is absolute.

In a democracy, citizens can gather to protest government policies and form committees and groups to lobby the legislative bodies to change laws. That does not happen in a kingdom. God's Word is absolute in His Kingdom, because it is set down for all to see in the Bible, which is the "constitution" of the Kingdom of God. The King has decreed that adultery is a sin. This is recorded in the "constitution" in Article Exodus, Section 20, Subsection 14: "You shall not commit adultery," and Article Leviticus, Section 18, Subsection 20: "Do not have sexual relations with your neighbor's wife and defile yourself with her." These decrees, and others like them, are stronger than stone because they are the words of the King. His Word is law and will never change.

If we claim to be living the Kingdom life, we cannot constantly be forming our own little groups to advance our own opinions or to challenge the Word of the King. As law, His Word is non-negotiable and immutable. We run into problems every time we try to carry our democratic mentality over into Kingdom life.

A Lesson From a Man Named Job

We would all do well to take a lesson from Job. A man greatly blessed by God in family and wealth, Job lost everything after God allowed satan to test his faith. Through much travail and suffering, including the worthless advice of some well-meaning friends, Job desired to debate God because he believed he was being treated unfairly.

That's when God stepped in to remind Job of his place and of the nature of their relationship:

Then the Lord answered Job out of the storm. He said: "Who is this that darkens My counsel with words without knowledge? Brace yourself like a man; I will question you, and you shall answer Me. Where were you when I laid the earth's foundation? Tell Me, if you understand. Who marked off its dimensions? Surely you know! Who stretched a measuring line across it? On what were its footings set, or who laid its cornerstone—while the morning stars sang together and all the angels shouted for joy?" (Job 38:1-7)

Here begins a dizzying barrage of questions that God puts to Job, running for four chapters and leaving him (and us) in no doubt regarding who is in charge. By the time it was all over, Job had changed his mind. He gained an entirely new attitude and a much humbler outlook:

Then Job replied to the Lord: "I know that You can do all things; no plan of Yours can be thwarted. You asked, 'Who is this that obscures My counsel without knowledge?' Surely I spoke of things I did not understand, things too wonderful for me to know. "You said, 'Listen now, and I will speak; I will question you, and you shall answer Me.' My ears had heard of You but now my eyes have seen You. Therefore I despise myself and repent in dust and ashes" (Job 42:1-6).

Job *repented.* He had a change of mindset that changed everything else. He began to see his life from a Kingdom perspective. We need to come to the same place and realize that we cannot fool around with God. He is the *King,* not the president. We did not vote Him in, and we cannot vote Him out. We need to lay aside our democratic mindset and start thinking like Kingdom citizens.

RETHINKING THE END TIMES

A vital part of healthy Kingdom thinking is having a clear and proper understanding of what Scripture says concerning the return of Christ and other apocalyptic themes. This is important because as Kingdom citizens we have a critical role in preparing for Christ's return. There is a lot of confusion and misinformation in the church on the issue of the end times. We have a responsibility to be well informed, based on what the Word of God actually says, and we must avoid at all cost the speculations and interpretations of today's prophecy teachers.

One day Jesus' disciples put to Him a question that people throughout the ages have pondered:

As Jesus was sitting on the Mount of Olives, the disciples came to Him privately. "Tell us," they said, "when will this happen, and what will be the sign of Your coming and of the end of the age?" Jesus answered: "Watch out that no one deceives you. For many will come in My name, claiming, 'I am the Christ,' and will deceive many. You will hear of wars and rumors of wars, but see to it that you are not alarmed. Such things must happen, but the end is still to come. Nation will rise against nation, and kingdom against kingdom. There will be famines and earthquakes in various places. All these are the beginning of birth pains. Then you will be handed over to be persecuted and put to death, and you will be hated by all nations because of Me. At that time many will turn away from the faith and will betray and hate each other, and many false prophets will appear and deceive many people. Because of the increase of wickedness, the love of most will grow cold, but he who stands firm to the end will be saved. And this gospel of the kingdom will be preached in the whole world as a testimony to all nations, and then the end will come" (Matt. 24:3-14).

WHEN WILL THE END COME?

This question seems to interest everyone, believers and nonbelievers alike. This passage from chapter 24 of the Gospel of Matthew is one of the favorite scriptures for those who are seeking information on the end times. It speaks of wars and rumors of wars, famine, earthquakes, false prophets, tribulation, hardship, and the increase of evil in the earth. Many preachers and teachers cite these events and point to current-day examples, and then proclaim, "The end is near! Do you see all these things happening around us?"

We need to be cautious and discerning when it comes to prophecies such as these and the people who proclaim them. Our generation is not unique; prophecy teachers have been around for centuries. Many of them are legitimate and are careful students of the Scriptures, but many others study the Word of God just enough to be frightening. They see "signs of the times" in every event, large or small. You hear them say: "Do you remember that earthquake in India? That means Christ is returning soon!" "The Lord said there would be pestilence and epidemics in the last days. With the scourge of AIDS spreading to so many people around the world, we know that Jesus' return is just around the corner."

What these teachers often fail to mention and many believers fail to see are Jesus' cautionary words in these verses. He says there will be "wars and rumors of wars, but *see to it that you are not alarmed. Such things must happen, but the end is still to come.*" Famines and earthquakes are merely "*the beginning of birth pains.*"

The *real* key to understanding the timing of the return of Christ and the end of all things is verse 14:

And this gospel of the kingdom will be preached in the whole world as a testimony to all nations, and then the end will come (Matt. 24:14).

The sign of the end of the age will be this: the preaching of the gospel of the Kingdom throughout the world. This verse reveals the *timing* of Jesus' return, but not the *hour*. It is quite clear that the *"hour"* is known only by the Father. Jesus Himself said, *"No one knows about that day or hour, not even the angels in heaven, nor the Son, but only the Father"* (Matt. 24:36). The end will come when the gospel of the Kingdom is preached "in the whole world as a testimony to all nations." The Greek word *ethnos* (nations) refers to every people group, every culture, every race, every tribe, every tongue, every political system, and every national state. After the gospel of the Kingdom is preached to all of these, then the end will come.

Who will do this? The answer cuts to the very heart of our dominion mandate. It is we, the believers and followers of Christ and the citizens of God's Kingdom, who bear the responsibility of proclaiming the gospel to the world. That is the commission that Jesus charged us with when He commanded, "Go and make disciples of all nations, baptizing them in the name of the Father and of the Son and of the Holy Spirit, and teaching them to obey everything I have commanded you" (Matt. 28:19-20a). When will Jesus return and the end come? When our commission is fulfilled. The specific *hour* of His return is in God's hands, but the general *timing* of it is in ours.

It is sad that we have spent so much time speculating on the hour of the return and so very little time on fulfilling the real sign that will usher in His return.

A KINGDOM KEY—
PREACH THE GOSPEL OF THE KINGDOM

If Jesus has not yet returned, it is because our commission to preach the gospel and make disciples in all the world has not yet been fulfilled. How many churches today are actively and conscientiously preaching the gospel of the Kingdom? They preach prosperity, they preach healing, they preach faith, they preach deliverance, they preach tongues, but how many preach the Kingdom of God? Not just any message will do. These are all legitimate themes but they are secondary when compared to the proclamation of the message of the Kingdom. Jesus will return only when the message of the *Kingdom* has been proclaimed in all the earth, and that proclamation is the Church's responsibility.

Generally speaking, the Church as a whole has fallen down on this responsibility. All we have to do is look around us to know this is true. Why do we have so many Muslims, Hindus, Buddhists, Shintoists, Scientologists, animists, atheists, and all of the other "ists" futilely searching for God? Why are there so many people who go through life with little or no knowledge of His Kingdom and what it can mean to them? It's because the Church hasn't done its job.

God knows what every person on earth needs and is looking for, even when we do not. The possibility of their salvation is contained in the Kingdom message. Throughout His earthly ministry, Jesus focused on preaching and teaching about the Kingdom:

Jesus went through all the towns and villages, teaching in their synagogues, preaching the good news of the kingdom and healing every disease and sickness. When He saw the crowds, He had compassion on them, because they were harassed and helpless, like sheep without a shepherd. Then He said to His disciples, "The harvest is plentiful but the workers are few. Ask the Lord of the harvest, therefore, to send out workers into His harvest field" (Matt. 9:35-38).

WHERE ARE THE WORKERS?

Jesus said that the harvest is plentiful. There is an abundant crop ripe and ready for the harvester's sickle. He was surrounded and followed everywhere by crowds of people who were "harassed and helpless," people who were wandering without hope or direction, people who were ripe for picking.

What was true in Jesus' day 2,000 years ago is still true in our day. Our world is filled with people searching for the truth, yearning for God, and stumbling in a gloom of spiritual darkness. There is nothing "wrong" with these people; they are still ripe for the picking. Whether they realize it or not, people want to get picked. Everyone wants to know that life has meaning and purpose and that they have a heavenly Father who loves and cares for them. We don't have to "ripen" a Buddhist or a

Hindu or a Muslim or anyone else for the harvest. They are already ripe, and have been for 2,000 years.

The problem lies not with the readiness of the harvest, but with the availability of harvesters. When Jesus said, "The harvest is plentiful but the workers are few," He was talking not only about *quantity* of workers, but *quality* of workers as well. A twofold problem exists: many believers who *should* be working in the harvest field are not, and many of those who *are* working are not doing a very good job. The entire world is ripe for the Kingdom of God, but we who are the citizens and representatives of that Kingdom are failing in our responsibility to bring in the harvest.

He appointed twelve…that they might be with Him, and that He might send them out to preach (Mark 3:14).

There is a time to sit at the feet of Jesus and enjoy His presence but there is also a time when we are sent out to preach this gospel of the Kingdom. Now is that time.

Many people who come into the Church get saved because they want "fire insurance." They want to make sure they don't go to hell. That's why we see so many backsliders, or spiritual dropouts. Someone gets afraid of the fire and comes to a meeting where a preacher tells him how to avoid hell by turning to Christ. Out of fear he runs to the front of the church, confesses his sins, accepts Jesus, gets his fire insurance policy, and calls it "salvation." After a couple of months he eventually becomes bored, frustrated, and depressed with this new "religion" thing and ends up going back into the world. Why? Because the world promises the very thing he expected to find in the Church but what the Church failed to deliver: power for living. The Kingdom of God is all about power, but many believers and others miss it because few churches truly teach it.

All of us want power in our lives. We all like to be in control. That is why we resist people's attempt to dominate us. It is why we hate to owe people money, because whoever we are indebted to controls us. We are looking for the power to control our circumstances. Humanity's quest for power is what makes the message of the Kingdom so appealing. The Kingdom of God represents power.

During His earthly ministry, thousands of people from all walks of life were attracted to Jesus—drawn to Him—because everything about Him spoke "power." He demonstrated power over sickness, power over nature, power over death, and power over sin. Everyone came to Him—rich, poor, it did not matter—because they felt powerless in their circumstances. Each one, in his or her own way, was looking for the Kingdom.

NICK AT NIGHT

Nicodemus, a respected Jewish religious leader, came to Jesus seeking the Kingdom. Jesus told him that he needed to be "born again" (see John 3:3). A rich young ruler came to Jesus seeking the Kingdom: "What must I do to inherit eternal life?" (Mark 10:17). He had money, but something was missing in his life. Jesus replied that he should give his wealth to the poor and "come, follow Me" (Mark 10:21). A Samaritan woman who had been through five husbands did not even know she was looking for the Kingdom until she met Jesus while drawing water from a well outside her village. There He told her of "living water" that He could give her that would satisfy her thirst forever and become "a spring of water welling up to eternal life" (John 4:10,14). She replied, "Sir, give me this water…" (John 4:15). In other words, she was asking, "How do I get into this Kingdom?"

People everywhere are looking for the Kingdom, even if they don't recognize it by that name. That is why the harvest is ready. All they need is for someone to show them the way. When I was in Malaysia, I could not preach Jesus publicly because it is a Muslim country. I was meeting with top people in the government for five hours every day and could not mention Jesus Christ as Savior and Lord. What could I do? I spoke to them about the Kingdom! When I was finished, everybody bought my tapes and books and I went home. Soon after, I began receiving E-mails from some of them saying things like, "I was reading your book, and I prayed the prayer…."

Some of these leaders were getting saved. Why? People are not looking for religion; they are looking for power, and the Kingdom offers power. The Kingdom represents the dominion we lost when Adam and Eve fell, and our nature drives us forward in a constant attempt to restore it. The harvest is ready. If we preach the gospel of the Kingdom of God, people will respond.

BALANCING LIFE, WHILE LIVING IN TWO KINGDOMS

Jesus began His public ministry with the words, "Repent, for the kingdom of heaven is near" (Matt. 4:17). As believers we face the daily challenge of living in two kingdoms at once: the Kingdom of heaven, where our citizenship lies, and the kingdom of this world, where we currently reside. The fact that these two kingdoms are often in conflict adds to the challenge.

As always, we should look to Jesus for an example of how to balance life in two kingdoms. One day, some of the Jewish religious leaders who opposed Jesus sought to trap Him with a question. It was a seemingly simple question that nevertheless could have backed Jesus into a corner had He not clearly understood the two-kingdom reality and the relationship between them.

> *Then the Pharisees went out and laid plans to trap Him in His words. They sent their disciples to Him along with the Herodians. "Teacher," they said, "we know You are a man of integrity and that You teach the way of God in accordance with the truth. You aren't swayed by men, because You pay no attention to who they are. Tell us then, what is Your opinion? Is it right to pay taxes to Caesar or not?" But Jesus, knowing their evil intent, said, "You hypocrites, why are you trying to trap Me? Show Me the coin used for paying the tax." They brought him a denarius, and He asked them, "Whose portrait is this? And whose inscription?" "Caesar's," they replied. Then He said to them, "Give to Caesar what is Caesar's, and to God what is God's." When they heard this, they were amazed. So they left Him and went away* (Matt. 22:15-22).

HAVING THE IMAGE OF A KING

Jesus' answer to His enemies' question was simple yet contained profound truth. As a Kingdom man, Jesus recognized that all governmental systems have legitimate claims and demands of their citizens. He simply said that we should give each kingdom its due. Every earthly kingdom has its own tax system. Because the coin used for paying the tax to Rome bore Caesar's picture, it meant that Caesar claimed it as his own. He was the king, and he was simply calling for that which was his. Whatever bore Caesar's image belonged to Caesar.

In the same manner, whatever bears God's image belongs to God. As beings created in the image of God, *we* belong to God, and He can claim us in a way no earthly kingdom can. The human leaders of the nation where we live and work and hold our citizenship may make legitimate claims on our time, our money, and our labor, but they have no claim on our character. We bear a deeper image and answer to a higher claim because we belong to God.

If "Caesar" asks for our money, we should give it because paying taxes is one responsibility of citizens of a free country, but if he asks for our first allegiance, that is where we have to draw the line.

DANIEL AND THE KINGDOM

In the Old Testament, no one wrote more about the Kingdom than Daniel. Although a Jewish exile, Daniel was also an important and high-ranking government official in the Babylonian empire. At the same time, he was a problem for the government because he understood Kingdom principles.

Once, Daniel ended up in a den of lions for refusing to obey the king's decree. The king demanded that the people pray exclusively to him for 30 days. Because Daniel worshiped and served God, he defied the king's order and was thrown to the lions as a result. God preserved his life by shutting the lions' mouths, and Daniel lived to serve his king for many more years. When the king overstepped his authority and demanded of Daniel an allegiance that was rightly due to God alone, Daniel quietly but deliberately refused. By his actions Daniel was saying to the king, "You command my time, my money, my labor, and, in matters of state, my allegiance, but you do not command my soul. My soul is stamped with a deeper image, the image of One who demands of me the highest allegiance of all."

THREE JEWS AND THE KINGDOM

Daniel also wrote of three other Jewish exiles who, like himself, were government officials and who also understood and obeyed Kingdom principles. Shadrach, Meshach, and Abednego steadfastly refused the king's order to bow down and worship an idol he had set up. As a result, they were cast into a blazing furnace that was so hot that it killed the men who threw them in. God protected them and delivered them safely from the flames, and they continued to serve Him and their king for many years (see Dan. 3). Their testimony was the same as Daniel's: In matters of the spirit, God demands undivided allegiance.

YOU AND THE KINGDOM

You may work in an office, and perhaps your boss comes to you asking you to do something that you know is not right. It may be unethical or even illegal. What should you do? If you are committed to Kingdom principles, you should respectfully but firmly remind your boss that although he can make demands of your time and your labor while you are on the job, he cannot make demands on your character. He may own the paper, the pencils, the paper clips, the computer, and even the company, but he does not own you. Stand up for what is right even if it puts your job at risk. Once you sell your character and integrity for the sake of your job, then your boss *will* own you. Remember that you have a deeper image on you and answer to a higher authority because you belong to another Kingdom.

Such is the challenge of living in two kingdoms. Each makes demands on us every day that require choices on our part. As long as those demands do not conflict, everything is OK. It is during the time when conflict arises that we show what we really believe and where our allegiance truly lies.

PRINCIPLES

1. As ambassadors of Christ, we represent our Father's Kingdom on earth.

2. We cannot be effective citizens of the Kingdom of God and continue to think democratically.

3. Right thinking always precedes right acting.

4. We need to lay aside our democratic mindset and start thinking like Kingdom citizens.

5. The end will come when the gospel of the Kingdom has been preached throughout the world.

6. The specific hour of Christ's return is in God's hands, but the general timing of it is in ours.

7. The problem lies not with the readiness of the harvest but with the availability of harvesters.

8. The Kingdom of God represents power.

9. People everywhere are looking for the Kingdom, even if they don't recognize it by that name.

10. As beings created in the image of God, we belong to God, and He can claim us in a way no earthly kingdom can.

11. In matters of the spirit, God demands undivided allegiance.

"*God made the country and man made the town.*"

THE ASSIGNMENT OF JESUS: RESTORE THE KINGDOM

Everybody in the world was born to fulfill an assignment. God created each one of us to solve a problem. There is something that God wanted accomplished that required our existence—every one of us. None of us are an accident. None of us are here by mistake. Our place on this planet is related to an assignment that God had in His mind long before the very existence of our world. This makes us critical to His global plan.

REVERSING THE CURSE OF MAN'S DEFECTION

God's purpose for us is the same as it has always been—to exercise dominion and authority over the earthly realm under His sovereign kingship. That has never changed. What *has* changed is our position. Adam and Eve's abdication of their rightful place of authority allowed satan, an unemployed cherub, to usurp the throne God intended for us to occupy. Relegated to the status of helpless subjects of a devastating kingdom of darkness, we cannot return to our original place without God's help.

Fortunately for us God did not simply write us off, wipe us out, and start all over. His eternal purpose will never be thwarted; His perfect will shall come to pass. From the very beginning, God had a plan that would resolve our defection: *"But when the time had fully come, God sent His Son, born of a woman, born under law, to redeem those under law, that we might receive the full rights of sons"* (Gal. 4:4-5). God's purpose was to restore us to our full status as His sons and daughters and bring us back into His Kingdom. He sent Jesus as the Way. Faith in Jesus Christ as the Son of God and in His death for our sins and resurrection for our life is the doorway through which we enter the Kingdom of God.

A KING AND HIS KINGDOM

Not only was Jesus the way into the Kingdom, but He was also the messenger who announced the arrival of the Kingdom on the earth. Before any of us could enter the Kingdom of God, we had to know it had arrived and where we might find the entrance. That is why Jesus came. Jesus' purpose was twofold: to proclaim the arrival of God's Kingdom and, through His blood, provide entry to the Kingdom for all who would come.

The Kingdom of God is central to His purposes in eternity. Everything God does relates to His Kingdom. Even in the physical realm, God's Kingdom was at the forefront in creation and will be the central focus at the end of time. Jesus said, *"This gospel of the kingdom will be preached in the whole world as a testimony to all nations, and then the end will come"* (Matt. 24:14). If the Kingdom is central to all that God is and does, it is only natural to expect that it would also be central to Jesus' mission and message. Indeed it was, as Scripture makes clear.

THE MISSION STATEMENT OF JESUS

Every successful organization, whether a business, a nonprofit group, a family, or whatever, needs a mission statement. Whether it is a formal written statement or simply an informal understanding, a mission statement should clearly define and crystallize the organization's purpose, philosophy, and goals. Every person in the organization should internalize and understand the statement so that all are working together to accomplish the mission. A mission statement helps keep everyone on course, which is important because the organization's product, service, or message will grow out of its mission statement.

According to the Gospel of Matthew, when Jesus initiated His public ministry, His first public declaration was a message that reflected the mission statement for His life: *"Repent, for the kingdom of heaven is near"* (Matt. 4:17). As we have already seen, *repent* means "a complete change of mind and thinking—a whole new mentality—and a complete change of life direction." The Kingdom of heaven refers to the sovereign presence and authority of God "invading" and impacting the earthly environment. Jesus challenged His listeners to change from a mindset that ignored or denied God's Kingdom to one that acknowledged and embraced its arrival.

Jesus' mission was to proclaim the Kingdom of heaven. This assignment from His Father reflects His mission statement, which He declared one Sabbath in the synagogue in Nazareth, His hometown: "The Spirit of the Lord is on Me, because He has anointed Me to preach good news to the poor. He has sent Me to proclaim freedom for the prisoners and recovery of sight for the blind, to release the oppressed, to proclaim the year of the Lord's favor" (Luke 4:18-19).

REINTRODUCING THE KINGDOM

More than simply revealing the Kingdom, Jesus' assignment was to *reintroduce* the Kingdom. He came to *bring* back to mankind a knowledge of the Kingdom of God, as well as to change their thinking so they might effectively live in that Kingdom. With a holy passion Jesus pursued this heavenly assignment. Before He returned to the throne of His Father, He trained His disciples to continue this mission until its ultimate conclusion. This Kingdom mandate has been passed from generation to generation with varying degrees of success. Unfortunately, much of the Christian Church has lost sight of the message of the Kingdom and preaches alternative religious themes.

This is a serious problem, particularly because fulfilling the assignment of preaching the Kingdom is the key to the timing of the return of Christ. Jesus said that the end will come after the gospel of the Kingdom is preached to all nations. Every tribe, culture, and people group must hear the gospel of the Kingdom before Jesus can return. The fact that Jesus has not come back yet is proof that His assignment, which He delegated to His followers in every generation, has not yet been fulfilled.

I have a problem with the people today who are preaching and prophesying that we are in the "last days" and that the Second Coming of Jesus is right around the corner. Let's consider the facts: Jesus will return after the gospel of the Kingdom has been preached to all the nations. Currently, the world population exceeds 6 billion. China alone has over 1 billion people, the vast majority of whom have never even heard the name of Jesus. Only 1 percent or less of the Chinese people are believers and followers of Christ. India's population has now crossed the

1 billion threshold. Approximately 98 percent of Indians are Hindu, Buddhist, or Muslim. Again, 1 percent or less believe and follow Christ. What this means is that in these two nations alone, more than 2.2 billion people do not know Christ, and most of them have never even heard the gospel.

Over 800 million people live in Africa, many of whom are animists. Many others are Muslim. Although Christianity is firmly established in Africa, many African believers have never heard the gospel of the Kingdom of God. They know Jesus, but they have never been taught about their status and rights as sons and daughters of God and citizens and heirs of His Kingdom.

Even in Europe and the West, including North and South America and the Caribbean, few people have heard the gospel of the Kingdom. Many have heard about Jesus, and a large portion of the people in these places are followers of Christ, but even many of these believers have never heard the Kingdom message. There is still much work to do before Jesus' assignment of preaching the gospel of the Kingdom to all the nations is fulfilled.

The Assignment of Jesus: Preach the Kingdom

Everywhere He went, Jesus preached the Kingdom. That was His assignment. Jesus primary message was not the born-again message that dominates gospel preaching. In His entire recorded ministry, Jesus spoke only once about being born again, and that was in the middle of the night to a Pharisee named Nicodemus who had come to Jesus privately. Being born again is the way into the Kingdom—it is the necessary first step. But the gospel of the Kingdom involves much more.

Not only did Jesus rarely speak about being born again, neither did He make these other themes the focus of His preaching: prosperity, healing, baptism in the Holy Spirit, or many of the other things we preach so much about today. Jesus *taught* about those things, and He demonstrated them in His day-by-day ministry, but He didn't *preach* them. There is a big difference. Jesus had only one message: the Kingdom of God. That was His assignment, and He passed it on to us. His assignment is our assignment.

He left the earthly realm in order to complete the work that He began. He sits on the throne of heaven directing that work through His representatives. Unfortunately, most of us do not really understand what Jesus meant when He spoke of the Kingdom. That is why we need to study closely His message so that we can preach it accurately and help fulfill His assignment in preparation for His return. As Jesus did, we need to proclaim that the Kingdom of heaven is near, that God is working to restore us to our original and rightful place as His children, as heirs to His Kingdom, and as rulers of the earthly dominion.

RESTORING OUR PLACE IN GOD'S PLAN

Why is preaching the gospel of the Kingdom of God so important? Why did Jesus focus so singlemindedly on that message? It all has to do with God's unchangeable purpose. From the beginning, God's intent has been to extend His heavenly Kingdom onto the earth through mankind. That remains His intent, despite the fall of man. At first, Adam and Eve were completely fulfilled, fellowshiping with God and exercising their dominion authority as He intended. However, their sin and disobedience caused them to forfeit their authority. They lost the Kingdom.

The gospel of the Kingdom reveals how God is restoring us to our place, how He is taking us back from where we came. This is an important point to understand. Many of us assume or have been taught that the gospel means that God is preparing to take us to heaven as our home. That is not true restoration, because we did not come from heaven. Restoration means to put back in the original place or condition. Since we fell not from heaven but from our dominion authority on earth, being restored means putting us back in our place of earthly dominion.

Imagine a book lying on a table. If that book falls to the floor and I pick it up and place it on a shelf, have I restored it? No, because I did not put it back where it came from, but placed it somewhere else instead. The book could not get itself back into its proper place; I had to reach down, pick it up, and place it there myself. In the same way, in our fallen state we could not regain our original place on our own. God had to come down, lift us up, and restore us to our former status.

WHERE IS OUR HOME?

Most of us have been taught to hope for heaven in the sweet "by and by." The only problem is that heaven is not where we came from. It was satan who fell from heaven, not man. We were made for the earth. God created us from the dust of the ground, breathed His life into us, and set us up as rulers over the physical realm. Ever since our fall He has been working His plan to restore us to the place from which we fell. Since we did not fall from heaven, it is not God's ultimate goal for us.

One of God's biggest challenges in getting His message of the Kingdom to the world is the fact that we who are His representatives on earth are so slow to understand the message. Dreams of golden streets and heavenly bliss have blinded us to our responsibilities on earth. We like to talk about heaven because, for us, it represents for us our highest goal and because it helps us get our minds off of our problems here in the earth realm. When we're busy singing "I'll fly away, O glory," and "When we all get to heaven, what a day of rejoicing that will be," it is easy to forget—for a little while—our car trouble, our overdue bills, the latest rent increase, or the job we just lost.

God's desire is to restore us to our former and rightful place, which means returning us to the position of authority and dominion over the fish, birds, cattle, plants, and all the rest of the earthly realm. As sinners we were slaves of satan in the kingdom of darkness, but as believers cleansed by the blood of Jesus we are sons and daughters of God in the Kingdom of light. All along God has desired not servants, but true sons and daughters who would be citizens of His heavenly realm and live in continual relationship with Him.

RELATIONSHIP VERSUS RELIGION

God is more interested in having daily communion with us than He is in our having "perfect" worship services where everything is exactly "proper" and where all our traditions and rituals are exactly in place. *Man wants religion while God wants a relationship.* We are easily impressed by religious rituals constructed on the foundation of an improper understanding of God's eternal purposes. Man seeks to relate to God through the principles of religion while God seeks to relate to man through the mystery of a personal relationship. It is clear that many do not have any real or deep relationship with the Lord because they do not understand the nature or significance of the Kingdom.

There was no "worship," at least, as we know worship, in the Garden of Eden. There were no altars, sacrifices, songs, clapping, dancing, Bibles, hymnbooks, sermons, or prayers—none of this stuff we call "religion." There was only relationship: Adam and Eve walking and talking with God in perfect fellowship and harmony.

Man fell from this intense passionate relationship with God, and God is seeking to restore man back to the simplicity of the Garden experience. Furthermore, our kingly authority over the earth is something He wants us to exercise and enjoy *now*, not just some distant day in the future after we have died and gone to heaven.

Kingdom thinking means recognizing that we do not have to resign ourselves to live in poverty, pain, suffering, and trouble "here below" until the Lord rescues us. We can claim and assert now our authority as sons and daughters of the King of the universe. We can experience the victory that is ours as people of the Kingdom.

THE KINGDOM IS NEAR

After all, Jesus did not say, "Repent, for the Kingdom of heaven is coming *someday*." He said, "Repent, for the Kingdom of heaven is *near*." His disciples thought the Kingdom was only for the future, but Jesus said, "No, because I am with you, the Kingdom of heaven is with you. When the Holy Spirit comes to dwell in you, the Kingdom will then be *in* you also."

Essentially, the Kingdom of heaven does not refer to physical territory. The Kingdom of heaven is a jurisdiction over which the influence of God has full authority. It is the "breakthrough" point where the Kingdom of God impacts the physical, earthly environment. In other words, the Kingdom of heaven is in my neighborhood because I live there and the Kingdom of heaven is in *me*. Because the Kingdom is in me, the house I own and occupy is the property of the Lord of hosts. As believers, we have the Kingdom of heaven in us. So wherever we go, and to wherever our influence extends, we bring the Kingdom of God into that place.

THE POWER OF AN AMBASSADOR

A parallel to this dominion authority is best illustrated in the function of ambassadors and embassies. Ambassadors are diplomats who carry out diplomacy for the government they represent. As Christ's ambassadors, we represent the Kingdom government of God. We are diplomats of His Kingdom in this world. Learning to see ourselves as ambassadors will change the way we think and live.

Whenever two nations establish formal diplomatic relations with each other, they open embassies in each other's capital city. The land on which each embassy is located is regarded as the sovereign territory of the nation whose embassy is located there. That sovereignty is recognized and respected by the government of the host nation as well as all other nations. In other words, for example, the United States' embassy in Nassau is American soil just as much as Miami, Washington, or New York. Even though it is located geographically on Bahamian soil, within its grounds the government of the Commonwealth of the Bahamas has no jurisdiction or authority.

If a Bahamian citizen or an American citizen, or a citizen of any nationality, is fleeing from local law enforcement and manages to get inside the U.S. embassy grounds, that person is safe from capture, at least for the moment. Because the embassy is United States territory, the Bahamian police cannot legally pursue the fugitive onto its grounds. The Bahamian government must employ diplomatic channels with the United States government to arrange for extradition.

That's how powerful an embassy is. Whatever area over which the authority of a government rests becomes that government's property. All the authority, rights, and powers of the nation represented by that government are in effect on that property. In the same way, we are ambassadors of Christ and of the Kingdom of God. Our home, office, church, and, indeed, anywhere our influence extends becomes an "embassy" of heaven. Leviticus 25:23 says that the land belongs to God and that we are merely strangers and sojourners here. We occupy land in a "foreign" country, but the property belongs to the government of heaven.

INFLUENCE OF AN AMBASSADOR

Whenever we are in the presence of an ambassador, we are in the presence of the government he or she represents. The words of the U.S. ambassador are the words of the United States government. Diplomatically speaking, they are one and the same. When we meet an ambassador, we are meeting more than just a person; we are meeting a nation.

As ambassadors of Christ, we represent our "home government"— the Kingdom of God. When people come into contact with us they should meet not just a person, but the God whom we belong to and who dwells inside of us through His Holy Spirit. If our spirit is in harmony with His Spirit in us, then what we say and do will reflect the government we represent and the Kingdom where we hold our citizenship.

The Holy Spirit is the key to our authority. As long as the Holy Spirit is inside a person and allowed to have control, then God's Kingdom can come; His rulership on earth can take place through that person. If the Holy Spirit departs, Kingdom authority departs with Him. That's what happened to Adam and Eve when they sinned. Without the Holy Spirit, they no longer possessed their dominion authority over the earth as God's vice-regents and were powerless to prevent satan from usurping the throne.

BREAKING DIPLOMATIC RELATIONS

Whenever a national government changes leaders, the new leadership recalls the old ambassadors, who no longer represent the government, and appoints new ones who will reflect the views and policies of the new administration. Sometimes, nations in conflict with each other sever diplomatic relations and recall their ambassadors. In a spiritual sense, this is what happened in the Garden of Eden. When Adam sinned, the kingdom of man entered into conflict with the Kingdom of God. The government of God broke diplomatic ties with man and "recalled" the Holy Spirit. Because of his sin, Adam became an unholy container and God withdrew His glory, His presence, and His ruling authority.

When man lost the Spirit of God, the Kingdom of God could not come fully on the earth. After Adam sinned, he was like an ambassador with no power, a man without a country, enslaved in satan's kingdom of darkness. From Adam to Jesus there were countless generations of human "ambassadors" who misrepresented God's government because they had no legitimate power or authority. In order for God's Kingdom to come on earth, some way had to be found to get the Holy Spirit back into man. Somehow, mankind's dominion authority and Kingdom citizenship had to be restored. Jesus came to earth to restore man to his rightful position in the universe.

There is a kingdom of darkness ruled by satan, and a Kingdom of light ruled by God. All of us were born into the kingdom of darkness. That is why we could not help sinning. Satan's power was now ruling instead of man. He had successfully reduced man to a state of impotency. Jesus came to destroy the works of the devil (see 1 John 3:8) and to deliver us from the kingdom of darkness into the Kingdom of light (see 1 Pet. 2:9) and give us power to take our rightful place.

Although we were once children of darkness, we are now children of light, and we should think and live accordingly: *"You are all sons of the light and sons of the day. We do not belong to the night or to the darkness"* (1 Thess. 5:5); *"For you were once darkness, but now you are light in the Lord. Live as children of light"* (Eph. 5:8). Jesus' goal was to cleanse us of our sin, to change us from unholy to holy vessels suitable for the Holy Spirit to reside in. *"But if we walk in the light, as He is in the light, we have fellowship with one another, and the blood of Jesus, His Son, purifies us from all sin"* (1 John 1:7). By doing this, it becomes possible for God to fully establish His Kingdom, a kingdom made up of His children who represent Him faithfully in the earth.

John 1:12 says that to everyone who believes in Him, Jesus gives the *power* to become children of God. We are used to trusting ourselves to control our lives. Most of us have done a pretty miserable job with that trust. Once we turn our trust toward God we are introduced to a new *power* to live our lives. That power also enables us to fulfill the commission as ambassadors of the heavenly Kingdom, a commission that He will never rescind. As true sons of God we are now connected to the government of God. Now begins the process of tutoring us to rule as royalty. This grooming process is the work of the Holy Spirit.

Preparing for the Holy Spirit

From Adam until Jesus, the Holy Spirit did not dwell inside anyone. He could not, because the government of God is holy, but the human vessels designed to carry it were unholy. Prior to Jesus, no sacrifice was ever offered that was good enough or sufficient to make us holy again. No one on earth was holy enough to provide a suitable dwelling place for the Spirit of God.

This does not mean that the Holy Spirit was not present and active during Old Testament days. On the contrary, the Bible records many instances of the Spirit's work during that time. However, a singular and significant difference exists between the Spirit's presence in the Old and New Testaments. In the New Testament, the Holy Spirit filled believers and came to live *in* them permanently. In the Old Testament, He only came *upon* certain individuals for a period of time and then departed. The Old Testament people of God did not know God's Spirit as a continually abiding presence in their lives. They only knew the exterior influence of the Spirit of God.

The Spirit *came upon* Samson and he performed mighty feats of strength. He *came upon* Moses and Elijah and Elisha, enabling them to do great signs and miracles. He *came upon* Gideon, who then defeated an army of thousands with 300 men. The Spirit *came upon* King Saul, who prophesied with the prophets. In each case, however, the Spirit came for brief season and then departed, because none of them were yet fit vessels for His abiding presence. None of them were able to execute the administration of God's Kingdom on an everyday basis.

A New Order Is Coming

Such was the situation until Jesus came. Although none of the Old Testament prophets experienced the Holy Spirit as an indwelling presence, some of them did receive glimpses of this future relationship. The prophet Joel wrote, "And afterward, I will pour out My Spirit on all people. Your sons and daughters will prophesy, your old men will dream dreams, your young men will see visions. Even on My servants, both men and women, I will pour out My Spirit in those days" (Joel 2:28-29). After Malachi, the last prophet in the Old Testament, there was a period of 400 years known as the "silent years," when no prophetic voice was heard in Israel.

This prophetic silence came to an end when John the Baptist appeared in the wilderness, preaching a message of repentance and proclaiming that the Messiah was coming soon. Although John appears in the four Gospels of the New Testament, he was in fact the last of the Old Testament prophets. His death at the command of Herod Antipas and the initiation of Jesus' public ministry marked the end of one era and the beginning of another. More specifically, the baptism of Jesus by John was the point of transference. From this point forward, a new order, the Kingdom of God, would be established. *"The Law and the Prophets were proclaimed until John. Since that time the good news of the kingdom of God is being preached, and everyone is forcing his way into it"* (Luke 16:16).

JOHN AND THE NEW WORLD ORDER

As great as John was, he still represented the old order. The arrival of Jesus inaugurated a greater period, the period of the Kingdom of heaven on earth. Jesus Himself said, *"I tell you the truth: Among those born of women there has not risen anyone greater than John the Baptist; yet he who is least in the kingdom of heaven is greater than he. From the days of John the Baptist until now, the kingdom of heaven has been forcefully advancing, and forceful men lay hold of it"* (Matt. 11:11-12).

"From the days of John the Baptist" the Kingdom had been "forcefully advancing" until it arrived with Jesus. Prior to John, the Kingdom had never been present on earth in such a powerful, visible state as it was with the coming of Jesus. No one from Abraham to John clearly understood the Kingdom. They talked about it and prophesied about it. They had little peeks into the future but never saw its manifestation in their times. John the Baptist preached about the Kingdom, but even John never accurately perceived the full implications of his own message. He witnessed its coming in Jesus, but never fully entered into it himself.

John was an Old Testament prophet with a New Testament revelation. He introduced the King who was to reintroduce the Kingdom, but he never experienced it for himself. The Kingdom was of a new era, and John was passing away with the old. John never received the Holy Spirit. He witnessed the Spirit coming down on Jesus at His baptism, but the indwelling Spirit was also a part of the new era that John would not experience to its fullest capacity. This is why Jesus said that, as great as John was, even those who were the least in the Kingdom of heaven were greater than he was.

John was a man who stood in the middle, suspended between two dimensions of time. His voice was a voice of preparation, preparing people to enter into this new order. Once Jesus' public work began, John's ministry came to an end. John understood this clearly. He understood that as Jesus' ministry increased, his must decrease until it eventually faded away. With the imprisonment of John we see the initiation of the ministry of Jesus. *"After John was put in prison, Jesus went into Galilee, proclaiming the good news of God. 'The time has come,' He said. 'The kingdom of God is near. Repent and believe the good news!'"* (Mark 1:14-15). Jesus began proclaiming His message of the Kingdom *after* John was imprisoned. The old order has now ended and the new order has commenced.

CITIZENS OF A NEW ORDER

After Jesus was baptized by John in the Jordan River and was "full of the Holy Spirit," the Spirit led Him into the wilderness where He fasted for 40 days and nights and was tempted by the devil. Emerging victorious from His temptation, "Jesus returned to Galilee in the power of the Spirit" (Luke 4:14) and began proclaiming His message of the Kingdom. Jesus was filled with the Holy Spirit without measure. Throughout the Gospels there is no evidence or record that while Jesus was on the earth the Holy Spirit was present or active anywhere else except in Him. He was the vanguard of a new order, the *first* of a new generation of people who would be filled with the Holy Spirit.

Jesus came to reconnect us to His Father and His glorious Kingdom. The connecting link is the Holy Spirit. That's why the focus of His message was: "Repent, for the Kingdom of heaven is near." Jesus' primary purpose was not to heal the sick, raise the dead, cast out demons, or perform other miraculous signs. Those things were only *signs* that the Kingdom of God had come to earth, but they were not His main focus. Jesus' ultimate assignment was to make way for the coming Kingdom by introducing men to the power of the Holy Spirit.

131

AN INVASION FROM HEAVEN

Calvary then becomes the gateway into this majestic Kingdom. The essence of the gospel is that we can get back our spiritual connection to our Father. There is now a power available to us so that we can fulfill our role in the advancement of the Kingdom into the earth regions. This power is made available to us through an invasion of the Holy Spirit into our lives. Jesus opens up the door for that invasion to happen.

Jesus promised that He would give us the Kingdom and the power to walk in that Kingdom. Jesus said, *"Do not be afraid, little flock, for your Father has been pleased to give you the kingdom"* (Luke 12:32). It is God's pleasure and desire to give us the Kingdom. He wants to restore our connection to Him. This is the heart of a loving Father: *"Which of you fathers, if your son asks for a fish, will give him a snake instead? Or if he asks for an egg, will give him a scorpion? If you then, though you are evil, know how to give good gifts to your children, how much more will your Father in heaven give the Holy Spirit to those who ask Him!"* (Luke 11:11-13)

Jesus' death on the cross was really a means to an end. Calvary became a cleansing fountain. Anyone who took the plunge into this fountain would become clean from the filth of living in this world. This cleansing would prepare them for receiving the power of the Holy Spirit.

After the work was done, Jesus appeared to His disciples and left this commission with them, *"Peace be with you! As the Father has sent Me, I am sending you."* After announcing their task, He breathed on them and said, *"Receive the Holy Spirit"* (John 20:21-22). With the cleansing process complete and now empowered by the Holy Spirit, the disciples were ready to go forward as His ambassadors, taking His Kingdom into all the world.

GOD COMES TO LIVE WITH MAN

Like those earliest disciples of Jesus, we who are believers have the Holy Spirit living in us as a continuing Presence. This makes us, like them, citizens of a new order. The authority and power we now possess as Spirit-filled ambassadors of the King gives us a taste of what Adam enjoyed before the fall. Our reconnection to the Kingdom of God is seeing Eden restored in our life and experience. With the Holy Spirit in control and leading us day by day, we can make wherever we are a little bit of "heaven on earth."

As citizens of the new spiritual order, we are greater than those Old Testament men and women who went before us. This is not because of any particular merit of our own, but because of the indwelling Spirit, which they did not know. To the extent that we have God's Spirit living in us, we are greater than Abraham. We are greater than Moses. We are greater than Samson, Samuel, and Saul. We are greater than David and Solomon. We are greater than Isaiah, Jeremiah, Ezekiel, Daniel, and all of the other prophets. They only talked about the Kingdom, but we are living in it.

Violence in the Kingdom

Again, in Matthew 11:12, Jesus said, "From the days of John the Baptist until now, the Kingdom of heaven has been forcefully advancing, and forceful men lay hold of it." In other words, ever since the days of John, an invasion has been under way. A military takeover is in progress, which no one knows about except those who have been captured. Have you been taken over? I have been taken over—by the Kingdom of heaven. It has taken over my heart, mind, soul, body, and my entire future. It has taken over my attitude and made me a dangerous man—to the kingdom of darkness.

The Kingdom of heaven is advancing forcefully, and we who are citizens of that Kingdom, as part of the "advance force" must continue to storm the stronghold of the enemy. The world may be against us, but we are able to effectively advance the Kingdom because we have a greater power living in us than the power that controls the world (see 1 John 4:4). Jesus said, *"In this world you will have trouble. But take heart! I have overcome the world"* (John 16:33).

We can be victorious by the power of the Spirit of God who resides in us. That is what it means to be citizens of the new order of the Kingdom of heaven. Gone are the days of rolling over and playing dead before the advances of the world. As Kingdom citizens we do not roll over and play dead for anyone; we advance forcefully. Gone are the days of wringing our hands over our problems, tribulations, and hardships. Gone are

133

the days of trying to overcome without going through. In spite of the affliction and opposition of the world we have learned to overpower the enemy by the power of the One who lives in us.

The Kingdom of which we are a part is so powerful that we need not fear any potential opposition. Kingdom men and women say, "Bring on the problems," and we will advance right through them. Our Kingdom does not run and it does not retreat; our Kingdom stands firm, advances, and overcomes.

REPRESENTING THE KING: THE POWER OF OUR POSITION

Understanding ourselves as ambassadors of Christ and representatives of His Kingdom relieves a lot of self-imposed pressure. Being Christ's ambassador is a wonderful privilege, but it also comes with tremendous responsibilities, which are:

- Speaking the words of the King;

- Being concerned with only the interests of the King; and,

- Speaking only on behalf of His government;

- Maintaining connection and communication with the King; and

- Carrying out the policies established by the King.

Although our call to be ambassadors of the King of the universe might seem overwhelming, the pressure of that responsibility is eased somewhat once we realize that all we have to be concerned with is speaking the words of our King. Jesus followed that course without exception, which is why He was so successful in His earthly ministry and example. He said, *"I do nothing on My own but speak just what the Father has taught Me"* (John 8:28b); *"My Father is always at His work to this very day, and I, too, am working. ...I tell you the truth, the Son can do nothing by Himself; He can do only what He sees His Father doing, because whatever the Father does the Son also does"* (John 5:17,19).

As ambassadors of Christ, we should be concerned only with the interests of our King. Everything we say and do should reflect desire and purpose. Our personal opinion does not matter. In the world of human diplomacy, an ambassador never shares his opinion. It is completely improper for an ambassador to express his personal opinion while acting in his official capacity as the representative and voice of his government. An ambassador who strays across the line into the territory of personal opinion risks jeopardizing his nation's reputation and possibly even its security, and sets himself up for possible censure and recall.

An ambassador who understands his role will simply communicate the position of his government, regardless of his private views. It is no different in the Kingdom of God. As ambassadors of our King, our opinion is not important. The only opinion that matters is that of the King. Often as believers we run into trouble because, having been raised in a democracy, we are too accustomed to giving our own opinions. Sometimes we even confuse our opinion with that of the King and end up misrepresenting Him by presenting our thoughts and ideas as His opinions, thus creating great confusion in the Church and in the world.

CARRYING OUT THE POLICIES OF THE KING

The only responsibility we have as Christ's ambassadors is to make sure we are connected to our King in such a way that we can know and understand what He says, and then speak and act accordingly. This is where the pressure is removed. We are not responsible for establishing policy; we are responsible only for carrying out the policies established by the King. It is not our job to decide what we believe and think. Our job is to learn and discern what our King thinks and then to come into agreement with Him.

Whenever someone tempts us or challenges us to take a position contrary to our King's will, all we have to do is fall back on what He said. Someone might ask, "What's wrong with a man and woman living together without marriage? What's wrong with sex outside of marriage? This is a new day and age, and we need to be up with the times." In response we can say simply, "Well, the position of my government (my King) is that it is sin." There is no debate, argument, nor ambiguity. We simply fall back on the Word of God and let the responsibility rest there.

As long as we concentrate on our King's interests and in representing Him faithfully, He will take care of ours. This He has pledged to do in a promise that can never fail. Jesus said as much when He told His disciples, *"So do not worry, saying, 'What shall we eat?' or 'What shall we drink?' or 'What shall we wear?' For the pagans run after all these things, and your heavenly Father knows that you need them. But seek first His Kingdom and His righteousness, and all these things will be given to you as well. Therefore do not worry about tomorrow, for tomorrow will worry about itself. Each day has enough trouble of its own"* (Matt. 6:31-34).

SUPPORT FROM THE HOME BASE

We should not focus on other things even in our prayers, but our concentration should be on the will of God and the coming of His Kingdom. An ambassador's home government provides him with everything he needs to live and perform his official function: office, home, car, staff, funding, etc. In the same way, as we seek God's Kingdom and His righteousness as our first priority, He will supply everything we need for daily living and accomplishing His will. If we set ourselves to handling our King's business, He will handle ours. It is a relationship of faith, trust, and obedience, enabling us to exercise power and authority in His name. Such faith grows from an increasing understanding of our position as ambassadors of Christ.

Jesus' assignment was to reintroduce the Kingdom of God on earth. He preached it and He demonstrated its reality and power through the signs and wonders He performed. He completed His mission by His death on the cross, offering His blood as a cleansing power to remove the influence and effects of sin in our lives. This cleansing of our lives makes us prepared to receive the Holy Spirit and connects us to the Kingdom of God. As His ambassadors, we have been charged to proclaim the message of the Kingdom to all the nations. The Church has experienced a mixture of success in its mission to the world because we have unfortunately created much confusion with our message. In order for the Church to effectively change the world she must clarify her message and commit herself to a renewed preaching of the gospel of the Kingdom.

CHAPTER FOUR

PRINCIPLES

1. Jesus' purpose was twofold: to proclaim the arrival of God's Kingdom and, through His blood, provide entry to the Kingdom for all who would come.

2. Jesus' assignment was to *reintroduce* the Kingdom.

3. Being born again is the way into the Kingdom—it is the necessary first step—but the gospel of the Kingdom involves much more.

4. The Kingdom of heaven is a jurisdiction over which the influence of God has full authority.

5. As Christ's ambassadors, we represent the Kingdom government of God.

6. The arrival of Jesus inaugurated the period of the Kingdom of heaven on earth.

7. Jesus' ultimate assignment was to get the Holy Spirit back into us.

8. As citizens of the new spiritual order, we are greater than those Old Testament men and women who went before us, not because of any particular merit of our own, but because of the indwelling Spirit, which they did not know.

9. The Kingdom of heaven is advancing forcefully, and we who are citizens of that Kingdom are part of the "advance force" that is storming the stronghold of the enemy.

10. Our Kingdom does not run and it does not retreat; our Kingdom stands firm, advances, and overcomes.

11. As ambassadors of Christ, we should be concerned only about the interests of our King.

12. As long as we concentrate on our King's interests and in representing Him faithfully, He will take care of our interests.

"There's many a good tune played on an old fiddle."

THE GOOD NEWS OF THE KINGDOM

E verything God does serves His Kingdom purposes. One of the main reasons we so often misunderstand God is because we fail to recognize this fact. From the beginning, God intended to extend His kingly dominion from the invisible and spiritual realm into the visible physical realm. This would be accomplished by ruling through human beings whom He created and placed in authority over the rest of the created order.

Because of sin, man abdicated his place of authority and came under satan's sway, falling into spiritual bondage and blindness. Since God's purposes never change, He enacted a plan formed from before the foundation of the world to help us rediscover His Kingdom. God's goal is to restore man to his rightful place of dominion and earthly leadership.

GETTING HEAVEN TO EARTH

Another way to say this is that God's purpose is to restore His rulership on earth *through* mankind. Satan the usurper must be removed from the earthly throne he stole. This restoration of God's rulership on earth through mankind is truly what lies at the heart of the faith we hold as believers and followers of Christ. It is what Jesus came to earth to accomplish in our lives. Jesus preached a very simple message: the Kingdom of heaven has come to earth. Jesus' message, which was given to Him by His Father, reflected His divine mission on earth, as well as the passion and desire of His heart. The driving motivation of Jesus' life was not to get us to heaven—that is the goal of "religion"—but to get heaven to us. Jesus' passion was to establish His Father's Kingdom *on earth* in the hearts of men.

We have heard so much in recent years about the increase of religious hatred, strife, and conflict around the world. Muslims have attacked and killed Christians, Jews, and Hindus as they burned churches and temples. Christians, Jews, and Hindus have done the same to Muslims, as well as to each other. Different sects of the same faith fight amongst themselves. All of this conflict leaves in its wake a backwash of death, despair, anger, hatred, resentment, bitterness, strife, disease, and poverty—all in the name of "serving God."

Do these devout militants serve the same God we serve? Many things are done in the name of God that are far from the Spirit of God. Unfortunately, the Christian Church throughout history has been far from blameless in this regard. Anytime the Church becomes obsessed with "advancing the Kingdom for Jesus' sake" to the point of abusing and even killing people, seizing other people's property, and fighting amongst ourselves, then we cease to accurately and effectively represent God in this world. We literally cease to be the Church. We may carry the name of Jesus, but we have strayed far from His Spirit.

God is not in the business of killing people, burning buildings, or destroying property. Advancing the Kingdom of God does not involve an invasion of physical territories. It involves an invasion into the inward parts of man's soul, capturing his heart and mind for the purposes of God. Our mission is not to overrun nations and take the people by the throat and shake them until they "see the light" and turn to Jesus. That's not the way God's Kingdom works. The Kingdom of God *has* invaded earth, but its target is human hearts, not geographical territory.

God does not need to conquer the earth because it already belongs to Him: "The earth is the Lord's, and everything in it, the world, and all who live in it" (Ps. 24:1). The Kingdom of God is not after the earth in the sense of owning property. The Kingdom of God is after the "world" that *affects* the earth—the world of human hearts and minds. Our kingdom is not of this world, but sin has blinded our eyes and we do not know who we are or where we came from. God wants to restore us to our former place of honor, dominion, and authority. He wants us to rediscover and reclaim our inheritance.

LEAVING AN INHERITANCE FOR THE NEXT GENERATION

Jesus came to reintroduce the Kingdom of God to us, and, through the offering of His life on the cross, provide the means by which we could enter into that Kingdom. A critical part of our introduction to the powerful truths of the Kingdom is about our inheritance as children of God. Matthew records a parable that Jesus introduced referring to that inheritance. The parable itself is about judgment and the distinguishing characteristics made between the righteous and the unrighteous. The King is sitting in judgment and has placed the righteous, pictured as sheep, on His right hand and the unrighteous, pictured as goats, on His left hand.

> *Then the King will say to those on His right, "Come, you who are blessed by My Father; take your inheritance, the kingdom prepared for you since the creation of the world. For I was hungry and you gave Me something to eat, I was thirsty and you gave Me something to drink, I was a stranger and you invited Me in, I needed clothes and you clothed Me, I was sick and you looked after Me, I was in prison and you came to visit me." Then the righteous will answer Him, "Lord, when did we see You hungry and feed You, or thirsty and give You something to drink? When did we see You a stranger and invite You in, or needing clothes and clothe You? When did we see You sick or in prison and go to visit You?" The King will reply, "I tell you the truth, whatever you did for one of the least of these brothers of Mine, you did for Me"* (Matt. 25:34-40).

KING, KINGS, AND A KINGDOM

Jesus is the King, but He is not our inheritance. Our inheritance is "the Kingdom prepared for [us] since the creation of the world." The gift that the King gives us is a Kingdom. We *inherit* the Kingdom, but Jesus *rules* the Kingdom. This Kingdom has been ours since the creation of the world. Adam and Eve knew and enjoyed that Kingdom in the Garden of Eden. Satan, however, deceived them into sin and stole their (and our) inheritance.

As our inheritance, the Kingdom belongs to us by legal right. Adam and Eve lost the "papers" in the Garden and forfeited the Kingdom benefits, for themselves and their future generations. Jesus came to remove satan from his illegal occupation of the throne and make it possible for us to reclaim our inheritance. He is, in a sense, the executor of our estate. Even though our inheritance has been waiting for us since the creation of the world, we must go through Jesus to receive it.

Suppose your father died while you were still a child, leaving you an inheritance of 10 million dollars and appointing me as trustee and executor. Even though the inheritance is yours, you cannot fully claim it until you reach the legal age of accession, or the age designated by your father in his will. As executor, I have the authority and responsibility to keep and administer the estate until the day arrives when it passes fully into your control. In the meantime, I stand between you and your inheritance, which makes me a mediator. Until you come of age, any benefits of your inheritance that you desire must come through me.

GETTING YOUR INHERITANCE

In the spiritual realm, Christ is the mediator between God and man. He stands between the Kingdom and us. He mediates between our inheritance and us. We cannot receive the full benefits of our inheritance unless we go through Him. Just as the 10 million dollars was ours as a child, even before we knew about it, even so is the Kingdom of God our inheritance from the foundation of the world.

Once you come of age, you come before me as trustee of your 10 million dollar inheritance and say, "I am now of age; I qualify. Give me the inheritance that my father left for me." All I then need from you is proof of your identification and that you have met the qualifications. Once I see that everything is in order, I cannot keep you from your 10 million dollars. It is yours, free and clear, and you have access to all the rights, privileges, and opportunities that it affords you.

Jesus says to us, "There is a great inheritance waiting for you, a Kingdom that is yours, even though you knew nothing about it. I am here to reveal it to you and help you claim it. I am the Mediator. I am the Door. Come to Me, trust in Me, and enter into the Kingdom prepared for you." When we take Jesus at His word, when we trust Him as the one who can cleanse us of our sin, when we give Him control and acknowledge Him as Lord of our lives, we meet all the "qualifications" necessary to receive our Kingdom inheritance.

THE FIRST STEP—BEING BORN AGAIN

Through Jesus we can enter the door of the Kingdom and begin to live and think and act like who we really are—children of the King. In the Gospel of John, Jesus refers to this step as being "born again."

That is exactly what being born again is—a step. It is an indispensable step, because we cannot get into the Kingdom without it, but it is only a step. Being born again is merely the first step of a whole new life, a journey of learning to know, appreciate, and experience our rights, privileges, and responsibilities as Kingdom citizens.

But if we spend all our time focusing only on that first step, we will miss many of the joys and blessings that lie beyond the door. There are many rooms in the house of God but we will miss experiencing the wonders of His Kingdom if we choose to go no farther than the front door.

LIFE INSIDE THE DOOR OF THE KINGDOM

Many believers get so completely fixated on Jesus as Savior and being "born again" that as soon as they are inside the Kingdom, they camp out on the doorstep and never go any farther. Jesus is the *doorway* to the Kingdom; but, believe me, there are more riches that await inside. Jesus Himself made this clear when He said:

I tell you the truth, I am the gate for the sheep. All who ever came before Me were thieves and robbers, but the sheep did not listen to them. I am the gate; whoever enters through Me will be saved. He will come in and go out, and find pasture. The thief comes only to steal and kill and destroy; I have come that they may have life, and have it to the full (John 10:7-10).

"Life...to the max"—that's what our Kingdom inheritance is all about, and it *begins* with Jesus. But it does not end at the door. Remember that life is a journey and that life in the Kingdom will require that you move beyond your original experiences with God and mature and grow as a true son of the Kingdom.

Claiming our inheritance is not about joining a particular church or denomination. It has nothing to do with being "religious." It has *everything* to do with understanding that we are citizens of a Kingdom established and ruled by God, which will endure forever. As Kingdom citizens, we have legal rights to the government. The reason so many of us receive so little from God is because we do not recognize ourselves as citizens of His Kingdom, do not understand our rights as citizens, and therefore lack the confidence or boldness to *ask*. Kingdom citizenship is a spiritual reality, but it is also a *mentality*. As believers, we already have the Spirit of God, but we need to learn the *mind* and the *heart* of God. We need training in thinking and living as God's children.

CITIZENS OF A NEW COUNTRY

Once we become believers and enter the Kingdom of God, we "change countries." We surrender our citizenship in the world to become naturalized citizens of the Kingdom of heaven. We are *in* the world but not *of* the world. We enter the Kingdom through Christ, who is the doorway. God accepts us, naturalizes us as Kingdom citizens, and then commissions us as ambassadors of His government so that we can help others find the doorway as well.

At work, at school, or wherever we go we must remember that we are Kingdom citizens residing in a foreign land, and the authority of our home government backs us up. All the rights, privileges, and benefits of our citizenship apply fully to us even though we reside in a foreign land. At any time we can call on the resources of our King, which are far more abundant than the resources of this world. When 5,000 people needed to be fed, Jesus' disciples saw only the limited resources of this world—five loaves of bread and two fish. Jesus, however, looked into His Father's pantry and saw enough to feed everyone and leave 12 basketfuls of leftovers.

Our Kingdom is one of abundant supply. We need to exchange our poverty mindset for a provision mindset. As long as we tend to our Father's business, He will provide everything we need. No matter what our situation, we can focus on the Kingdom, claim our Kingdom rights, and say with confidence, "My God will supply."

WHAT GOSPEL ARE WE PREACHING?

If the Kingdom of heaven is so full of promise and power and provision—if it is truly such "good news"—why aren't more people around the world rushing to get in? Everyone wants to know that they have the power in life in order to overcome the tragedies of life as well as discovering the ability to rise up and meet the challenges confronting us every day. We all long to know that our lives have meaning, purpose, and hope.

Everybody wants to discover his destiny and the power to make his dreams come true. The gospel of the Kingdom of God promises all of this and more, yet the vast majority of the world's people have not discovered it, much less embraced it. Why not?

- They have not heard the message of the Kingdom.
- Their minds have been blinded so they cannot see the Kingdom.
- They have heard the wrong message of the Kingdom.

There are many reasons. For one thing, many people simply have not yet heard the gospel because no one has preached it to them. Another reason is that satan has blinded the spiritual eyes and deafened the spiritual ears of countless millions so that they cannot hear or understand the gospel even when it is preached. There is a third reason that is perhaps the most serious of all: *the Church is preaching the wrong message.*

Matthew, in his Gospel, refers to the "good news of the Kingdom" and the "gospel of the Kingdom." Mark speaks of the "gospel of God," while Luke uses the phrase, the "good news of the Kingdom of God." To what specifically are they referring?

All these biblical phrases, although slightly different, have the same meaning. The word "gospel" means "good news." The Greek word for *gospel* is *evangelion,* from which we derive the words "evangelism" and "evangelist." *Evangelion* means "good news" or "good report." Evangelism, then, is the process of communicating good news, and an evangelist is an instrument for communicating that good news. By this definition, any good news is "gospel." If I informed you that you had inherited 10 million dollars, that would be "gospel"—good news—to you.

THE GOSPEL OF THE KINGDOM

The gospel of the Kingdom of God that we are called to preach as believers must be carefully defined so that there are no ambiguities.

Strictly speaking, the "gospel" is not the message itself but rather a *description* of the message. We were commissioned by Jesus to proclaim the message of the Kingdom of God, and that message is described as *good news* for everyone who hears its message.

Jesus never told us to go and simply preach a "gospel." There are many kinds of good news we could talk about. But there is only one that Jesus identified as the focus of our preaching. He told us to preach the gospel *of the Kingdom*. He even set the example for us by making this the focus of His own message. Remember that when Jesus began His public ministry, His first recorded words were, "Repent, for the kingdom of heaven is near" (Matt. 4:17). With those words, Jesus set the standard and the model for us to follow.

Jesus proclaimed the *good news* that the Kingdom of God had come to earth once again. That was His gospel. It was not news about a new religion or denomination. We weren't called to make people feel good with a message that created a warm fuzzy feeling. Jesus' message was the good news that God's Kingdom had come on earth and any who would come would be reunited in spirit and fellowship with Him and be restored to their full position and rights as children of God and citizens of His Kingdom. The *good news* of the Kingdom is that we can regain what Adam lost. We can once again assume the place of dominion authority that God intended for us from the beginning.

Jesus preached the gospel of the Kingdom of God. That is the *only* gospel He preached. Therefore, as far as we are concerned as believers and followers of Christ, the gospel of the Kingdom of God is the only *true* gospel. In other words, for us there is no good news other than the awesome and powerful news of the Kingdom of God. This message of the Kingdom is the only legitimate message we have to communicate to the world.

UNCHANGING PERSON AND THE UNSHAKABLE KINGDOM

One of our biggest problems in the Church is that we have gotten caught up in preaching something the Lord never told us to preach. He told us to preach the good news of the *Kingdom*, yet we have exclusively focused our preaching on Jesus as the door. We preach His death on the cross for our sins and His resurrection as the guarantee of our eternal life. All of this is indeed true, and it is certainly good news, but it is not the full gospel Christ told us to preach. He told us to preach the Kingdom. Jesus is the one who came to proclaim the Kingdom, and the one who through His death provided us entrance to the Kingdom. But we have become so engrossed in preaching about the door that we have never gotten around to talking about life inside the door. This is the message Jesus commanded us to preach. Jesus is the King who rules *over* the Kingdom. We need to let the world know that there is a Kingdom they can enter that will radically change the total order of their life.

One of the reasons the Church is not more effective at reaching the nations is because we are not preaching the message they need to hear. People all over the world are looking for the Kingdom of God, even if they are not aware of it. Everyone wants power. Unfortunately they have sought to get that power through money or status in life. These things, as many are discovering, do not give you the power you are really seeking. They don't give you the power to create happiness or control the negative influences in your life. In her very hands the Church has the message that will lead people to the power they are looking for. That message is the gospel of the King and His Kingdom. Unfortunately many in the Church have discovered the King but they have no clue about the Kingdom that He came to bring to mankind.

People will respond to the message that there is a Kingdom of life, power, authority, and joy that is freely available to them. This Kingdom is the answer to all of their dreams. It is the source of the power they are looking for. The Kingdom of God will give them courage to face and overcome all the pressures of living in a post-modern world. It is sad that a great percentage of Christians have not experienced the realities of the Kingdom of God, much less committed themselves to the broadcasting of its message.

WHAT DID JESUS PREACH?

When Nicodemus sought out Jesus by night to question Him privately, he was not really looking for a person; he was looking for a

Kingdom. He had recognized the power of God at work in the life and activities of Jesus, and it stirred his curiosity. He realized that Jesus had tapped into a dimension of spiritual reality that he had never experienced.

> *Now there was a man of the Pharisees named Nicodemus, a member of the Jewish ruling council. He came to Jesus at night and said, "Rabbi, we know You are a teacher who has come from God. For no one could perform the miraculous signs You are doing if God were not with him." In reply Jesus declared, "I tell you the truth, no one can see the kingdom of God unless he is born again.""How can a man be born when he is old?" Nicodemus asked. "Surely he cannot enter a second time into his mother's womb to be born!" Jesus answered, "I tell you the truth, no one can enter the kingdom of God unless he is born of water and the Spirit. Flesh gives birth to flesh, but the Spirit gives birth to spirit. You should not be surprised at My saying, 'You must be born again'"* (John 3:1-7).

In effect, Nicodemus was saying, "I see the Kingdom of God at work in You. How can I get it?" Jesus responded by telling Nicodemus how to *enter* the Kingdom—by being *born again*. In verse 3, when Jesus says, "No one can see the Kingdom of God unless he is born again," the Greek word for "see" (*eido*) means to see in the sense of knowing, perceiving, or understanding. Jesus states explicitly in verse 5 that without being born of the Spirit, "no one can enter the Kingdom of God."

Jesus spoke of being born again in response to Nicodemus's inquiry. There is no biblical evidence, however, that Jesus ever made the "born again" message the focus of His message to the crowds who thronged Him everywhere He went. The heart of Jesus' message was not about being born again; He preached about the Kingdom of God. He rarely spoke about the cross or so many other issues that have filled the place in our sermons. He did teach on these things with His own followers and others who came seeking more knowledge. His message was quite different when dealing with the scribes and Pharisees who challenged Him. But with the common people, Jesus preached the Kingdom of God.

THE KINGDOM IS PREACHED IN WORD AND DEMONSTRATED IN POWER

Jesus described the essence of the Kingdom in the various stories that He told the people. These stories are rich in symbolism and truth as He majestically portrayed the nature and characteristics of the Kingdom of God. In these creative stories He displayed the character of those who belong to this Kingdom. The nature of Jesus' proclamation was not just in the words He spoke. It was demonstrated in the power emanating from His life. The power of the Kingdom was demonstrated through Jesus by the miracles, signs, and wonders He performed. Crowds of people were drawn closer to the Kingdom by the words and actions of Jesus. The ones that "got the message" eventually became His followers and were introduced into fuller knowledge of who Jesus was and of how to enter the Kingdom through faith in Him.

When we preach Christ without preaching also about the Kingdom of God, we do people a great disservice. In reality, the two are inseparable. You cannot divorce the King from His Kingdom. It is really quite unfair to tell the world about Jesus Christ and the door that has been open to them without telling them about life on the other side of the door. It won't make sense. If we move forward and tell them about the Kingdom, that's another matter. When we tell them of a domain where there is life, hope, peace, joy, and the power to rise above daily problems and difficulties *right now*, and live successfully and victoriously *right now*, they will say, "Hey, I can relate to that! I can understand that." As the church we must complete the message of Christ by focusing on the Kingdom of God, which was the heart of the words of Jesus.

Let's face it, life is hard and full of suffering and pain. We live in a world of great anxiety. Terrorism, economic collapse, political confusion, unemployment, divorce, despair—people *need* good news. The Kingdom of God is that good news. It is the lost message of Jesus that needs to be resurrected in our times.

Why would little children run up to Jesus? Why would rich and poor alike follow Him? Why would more than 5,000 people hang out with Him for three days, enduring hunger just to see and hear Him? Why would men, women, and children leave their farms and fishing boats, shops, homes, and villages just to sit at His feet? Why would they suspend their livelihood for a time to rush out to the countryside when they heard He was nearby?

It was because they loved what He had to say. It was because He told them about citizenship in a Kingdom that would give them a higher lifestyle and greater future than they would ever find in any of the kingdoms of men. Jesus modeled the very message that He preached and it drew men and women from every strata of life. This is a great challenge to us in our times. The message that we preach must be the message that we live.

The most effective way to reach people is to first whet their appetites with the good news of God's Kingdom. After they know about the Kingdom and desire it for themselves, then explain to them how to get into it by trusting Jesus Christ to cleanse and save them from their sins and by yielding their lives to His control. A person must get into the Kingdom before he or she is ready for the deeper things—the kinds of things that Jesus taught His disciples privately.

That is why Jesus taught the people using parables. Those who had no interest in the things of God simply regarded Jesus' parables as nice stories with practical morals. On the other hand, for those who were genuinely searching for truth, His stories struck a responsive chord in their hearts that drew them to Him and stirred them to find in Him the answers they were seeking. Through Jesus they gained entrance into the Kingdom, where they were then free to explore every room and discover every benefit and pleasure that it had to offer.

A PERVERTED GOSPEL

"The Kingdom of God has come to earth. Let all who will, repent and enter in." That is the gospel that Jesus preached and commissioned His followers to preach. Somewhere along the way, the Church has lost its focus. Rarely in these days will we hear the message of the Kingdom being preached in our pulpits. We preach about so many other issues, but hardly at all about the Kingdom. We preach about prosperity, faith, gifts, ministries, and other secondary issues, but we don't preach the Kingdom.

Satan has sidetracked us. One of his most effective strategies is to preoccupy us with secondary things rather than the primary. The devil is smart. He knows better than to try to get us to do things that are blatantly wrong or evil. Instead, he turns our focus onto things that, although important, are not what the Lord has told us to focus on.

If we do something good that is not what the Lord told us to do, are we right or wrong? Suppose you employed me as a chef in your home, and in planning for a large dinner party asked me to prepare a turkey with all the trimmings. What if you led your guests to the table only to discover I had cooked a pot roast instead? Was I right or wrong? That pot roast might be the juiciest, tastiest, and most succulent pot roast you ever put in your mouth, but it was still not what you asked for. We have a tendency to believe that as long as something is not wrong, it must be right. However, even right things are wrong if they are done at the wrong time or in place of some other right thing that should have been done instead.

Two thousand years ago, Jesus was very clear in the assignment He gave to the Church. He left nothing to uncertainty or interpretation. He specified what we were to preach and teach:

> *Therefore go and make disciples of all nations, baptizing them in the name of the Father and of the Son and of the Holy Spirit, and teaching them to obey everything I have commanded you. And surely I am with you always, to the very end of the age* (Matt. 28:19-20).

> *Go into all the world and preach the good news to all creation* (Mark 16:15).

> *And this gospel of the kingdom will be preached in the whole world as a testimony to all nations, and then the end will come* (Matt. 24:14).

The New Testament proclaims all kinds of "good news" (gospel, *evangelion*). The good news that Jesus preached, and that we should preach, is that the Kingdom of God has come to earth and, through Jesus, we can all become part of it.

We have gotten so sidetracked on secondary and peripheral issues. It seems that the message of the Kingdom has all but disappeared. There is no doubt that Jesus Christ died on the cross that we might be forgiven of our sins and find eternal life in Him. There is also no doubt that we need to tell people that He is the Way, the Truth, and the Life, and that He is the *only* way to eternal life. All of this is *part of* the message of the Kingdom, but it is not *all* of the message. The cross of Christ is the *beginning* point of life in the Kingdom of God, not the ending point. There is no ending point, because life in the Kingdom has no end.

Our problem is that we spend so much time telling people how to get into the Kingdom that we rarely teach them what to do once they get inside. Often we don't know ourselves because no one has ever taught us, either. We spend so much time preaching about the door that we forget all about the palace behind it.

Stuck at the Door

We need to get back on track preaching the gospel that Jesus told us to preach—the good news of the Kingdom of God come to earth. God wants us to have the Kingdom, and Jesus is the way in. Jesus Himself said, *"Do not be afraid, little flock, for your Father has been pleased to give you the kingdom"* (Luke 12:32). Think of it! Our Father is *pleased* to give us the Kingdom. It is what He wants to do. It is what He has intended from the very beginning.

If we think of the Kingdom of God as a glorious palace or mansion, we have totally missed the message. We are stuck at the door. What is the purpose of a door? It provides entry into the house or into the different rooms of the house. In the same way, Jesus provides us with entry into the Father's Kingdom. Jesus said, "I am the Way." A door is a portal through which we pass from one place to another. Jesus is the door through which we pass from death into life, from darkness into light, from guilt into pardon, from shame into joy, from strife into peace, and from defeat into victory. Such is the contrast between the kingdom of the world and the Kingdom of God.

If we get "stuck" at the door, we will never experience the fullness of the Kingdom that the Father has prepared for us. We have to step beyond the doorway so we can discover a whole brand-new world of the riches and glory that lie within. Remember that Jesus said, *"I am the gate; whoever enters through Me will be saved. He will come in and go out, and find pasture...and...life to the full"* (John 10:9-10). The Kingdom is a place where we can experience life to the max.

Can you imagine someone inheriting a marvelous estate with a beautiful mansion and so fixating on their love for the door that they never step inside? "I love you, door! You're such a beautiful door. You have such graceful panels, such lovely glass. You are so wonderful!" Jesus is our door into the Kingdom of God. It is vitally important that we place our faith in Jesus to save us and forgive our sins, but it is just as important that afterward we move through the door so that we can participate in and enjoy the Kingdom to the fullest.

Jesus said, *"I am the gate for the sheep"* (John 10:7), but He also said, *"I am the good shepherd...[who] lays down His life for the sheep"* (John 10:11). Shepherds take care of their sheep. They lead them, protect them, and take them to places where they can find food and water. Shepherds do not *give* their sheep grass; they lead the sheep to where *the sheep* can find good pasture. Jesus is greater than King Arthur, and His Kingdom is more glorious than Camelot.

Jesus is the shepherd who brings us into the abundant pastures of His Father's Kingdom, but how much nourishment and refreshment we receive there is up to us. The Lord will not force-feed us. He wants us to participate fully in the joys and benefits and blessings of His Kingdom, but He will not violate our will. The degree to which we enjoy our Kingdom citizenship depends upon the degree of our willingness to be bold and claim what is rightfully ours—what Jesus has restored to us through His death and resurrection.

Unfortunately too many are stuck in the outer court and have never been able to journey beyond the outer perimeters of God's glorious Kingdom. They have never ventured into the most holy place where the King lives and where His Kingdom is fully manifested.

Imagine for a moment that you own a shoe store that specializes in expensive, elegant, stylish, and fashionable shoes of only the highest quality. You have invested a couple of million dollars to build an elegant and beautiful store and have spent thousands more to obtain the highest quality inventory of shoes available. Your desire is to reach the highest possible number of people with the news of the excellent shoes they can find in your store. What would you do? You would advertise, of course. Advertising is a form of preaching; you are spreading the "gospel"—the "good news" about the shoes you have for sale.

Suppose your advertisement ran like this: Hello. I want to invite you to visit us at Shoe World International, where you will find only the finest footwear for the entire family. I am confident that you will fall in love with our store, and particularly our door. We have a beautiful door made of solid oak overlaid with gold and fixed with sterling silver hinges. An elegant window of mirrored and beveled glass is set into the top half of the door. The door is eight feet high and six feet wide, a truly awesome and magnificent door. I am telling you, friends, that you don't want to miss this door. It will mesmerize you. You simply will not believe the beauty of our door until you see it. Come on down. We are looking to see you soon!

How many shoes do you think you would sell with an ad like that? How many customers would you draw into your store? You might get a crowd of curious people who come to look at your door and then walk away chuckling and shaking their heads, but you won't make much money. The object of advertising is to get customers *past* the door and into the store where they can see the merchandise you have available for them to buy.

It is the same with the Kingdom of God. We have not fulfilled all that the Lord desires for us until we move fully inside and avail ourselves of all that the Kingdom has to offer us. Only then can we begin to fulfill all the potential God has placed inside us. Yes, Jesus died for us, but He died to obtain something for us: entrance into the Kingdom of His Father. Jesus said, *"I am the way and the truth and the life"* (John 14:6). The life He gives us is the life of the fullness of His Kingdom, a Kingdom that has everything we could ever need or want, a Kingdom of overabundant and inexhaustible supply.

EXPERIENCING HEAVEN ON EARTH

John the Baptist, the Old Testament prophet with a New testament revelation, preached the Kingdom of God: "In those days John the Baptist came, preaching in the Desert of Judea and saying, *'Repent, for the kingdom of heaven is near'* " (Matt. 3:1-2). After John, Jesus came upon the scene preaching the same message: "After John was put in prison, Jesus went into Galilee, proclaiming the good news of God. *'The time has come,'* He said. *'The kingdom of God is near. Repent and believe the good news!'*" (Mark 1:14-15); "From that time on Jesus began to preach, *'Repent, for the kingdom of heaven is near'*" (Matt. 4:17). Where is the Kingdom? It is only a step away from where you are standing.

The good news that John and Jesus preached—and that the early Church preached—was the good news of the *Kingdom* of heaven. So much of the time today we get the message wrong by preaching the good news of *heaven*. The two are not the same. We tell people to put their faith in Jesus for salvation and then we focus on heaven as our goal and destination. Jesus never preached heaven. His disciples never preached heaven, and neither should we. There may be a lot of appeal to the idea of going to heaven in the "sweet by-and-by," but people struggling with daily life on earth need a message to help them in the "sour now and now." People need to hear the good news of the Kingdom of heaven—the rule of God has come to earth and all can experience the reality of that world.

ESCAPING THE WORLD OR CHANGING THE WORLD

There may be a lot of appeal to the idea of going to heaven in the "sweet by-and-by," but people struggling with daily life on earth need a message to help them in the "sour here and now." They need to be taught how to live in the world, not how to escape from the world.

Over the centuries an emphasis on heaven developed in the gospel message of the Church that was not there originally. Whenever mankind faces catastrophic events, he begins thinking about heaven—a place of escape, repose, and comfort. For Europeans that catastrophe was the black plague; for Africans it was slavery. Under both circumstances life expectancy was short, future prospects seemed limited, and the brevity and fragility of life became very real and personal to people. During the black plague, millions died in Europe, and many of the survivors turned to the hope of heaven as consolation. Under the cruel yoke of slavery, millions of Africans, bereft of any hope in this life, also turned to heaven as their future hope.

If everyone around you seems to be dying and you know you could be next, you tend to hold lightly to the things of this world and cling to the hope of the world to come. If you realize that you own nothing of your own, but that someone else owns you and everything you have, including your spouse and children, and all you have to look forward to each day is backbreaking labor, then a promise of permanent rest beyond brings strong comfort. The consequence of this kind of preaching is that all we can say is, "Just hang on. Things are tough, but the Lord is coming back, and when He does, He will take us all out of this mess."

Overcoming the World

The comfort of heaven helps to keep us and sustain us through dark hours, but it is not and should never be the focus of the gospel we preach. Scripture promises us not that Jesus would rescue us from a world on the brink of overcoming us, but that in Him we would overcome the world: *"I have told you these things, so that in Me you may have peace. In this world you will have trouble. But take heart! I have overcome the world"* (John 16:33); *"For everyone born of God overcomes the world. This is the victory that has overcome the world, even our faith. Who is it that overcomes the world? Only he who believes that Jesus is the Son of God"* (1 John 5:4-5).

What this means is that when we live and think and act like Kingdom citizens, we can experience success, victory, and fruitfulness, not in the "sweet by-and-by," but today, this week. It means that we can overcome *right now*. We don't have to be or remain victims of our circumstances. We can avail ourselves of our Kingdom citizenship and all its blessings, rights, and benefits to help us rise above our circumstances, either to change them, or to prosper and move forward in spite of them. Kingdom living does not sit back meekly in submission and defeat before the onslaught of the world. Kingdom living moves forward with confidence, advancing forcefully in the wisdom, power, and boldness that are ours as children of God.

Nothing outside of us is bigger than what is inside of us. That is what John meant when he wrote, *"You, dear children, are from God and have overcome them, because the one who is in you is greater than the one who is in the world"* (1 John 4:4). That is an unbeatable formula for victory. If we are being overcome by the world, then we are not experiencing what the Lord wants us to have. Something is missing. If life is beating us, then either we have gotten the wrong good news, which is the same as bad news, or we have gotten no news at all. The good news is that in Christ we are citizens of the Kingdom of heaven, and all the resources of that Kingdom are available to us to help us live in victory on a daily basis in the here and now.

THE ONLY TRUE GOSPEL

The gospel of the Kingdom is the only true gospel. Anything else we preach is not the true gospel, or at least, not the complete gospel. Preaching about Jesus Christ is a vital and essential part of preaching the gospel of the Kingdom, because He is our way into the Kingdom. Just because we place our faith in Christ, however, does not mean that we automatically understand either what it means to be a citizen of the Kingdom or how to live like one. There are many believers who trust and love Jesus but have never been taught about the Kingdom or their true and rightful place in it.

Jesus preached the gospel of the Kingdom of heaven, but His message had nothing to do with our going to heaven. As a matter of fact, He preached the opposite. Jesus preached that heaven was coming to earth; indeed, that it was already here, and He was its herald. He emphasized this even when He taught His disciples to pray: "This, then, is how you should pray: *'Our Father in heaven, hallowed be Your name, Your kingdom come, Your will be done on earth as it is in heaven'* " (Matt. 6:9-10).

THE PRAYER OF JESUS

First of all, Jesus said, "Our Father." He is not mine or yours alone, but the Father of all who believe. Secondly, our Father is "in heaven." He is not on the earth, but rules His Kingdom in heaven. When we pray we should address Him as being in heaven rather than on earth. Heaven, however, is not far away. It is the adjacent realm to our own. Any believer who dies is instantaneously there. That's how close God is. Jesus then teaches us to respect and honor God: "hallowed be Your name." *Hallowed* means "holy," and *holy* means "pure and without any ulterior motive;

separated, set apart from any and all evil." God means exactly what He says, and He always keeps His word.

Next come the words, "Your kingdom come, Your will be done on earth as it is in heaven." Notice that we are to pray for God's Kingdom to *come* (not go), as well as for His will to be done. The phrase "on earth" refers to both God's Kingdom and His will. The word *will* also means "purpose." When we pray for God's will to be done on earth, we are asking Him to carry out His purpose, to fulfill His original intent. We are praying that whatever happens in heaven will be manifested in the earth regions. When Adam fell he created a new phenomenon in the earth—a will other than the will of the Father. The focus of Kingdom men and women is to unite the world again under the one will of the Father.

God's original purpose was to extend His heavenly rule to earth through human beings. His desire was that our physical earthly realm would reflect His spiritual heavenly realm. Because the Kingdom of heaven on earth was God's original and unchanging intent, it was also the focus of Jesus' message and ministry. The four Gospels together contain over 100 direct references to the Kingdom. John the Baptist preached the Kingdom. Jesus preached the Kingdom; it was His only message. Peter, James, John, and the other apostles preached the Kingdom. Paul preached the Kingdom. The early Church preached the Kingdom.

A dark and weary world, hopeless and despairing, awaits—and desperately needs to hear—the good news of the Kingdom of God. By preaching the gospel of the Kingdom to all nations, we prepare the way for the return of Christ. That is our mission, our assignment as the Body of Christ. If we do not preach it, who will?

PRINCIPLES

1. God's purpose is to restore His rulership on earth *through* mankind.

2. Jesus came to reintroduce the Kingdom of God to us and, through His shed blood on the cross, provide the means by which we could enter into it.

3. As an inheritance, the Kingdom belongs to us by legal right.

4. We proclaim the message of the Kingdom of God, and that message is *good news* for everyone who hears it.

5. Jesus never preached about being born again; He preached about the Kingdom of God.

6. The good news that Jesus preached, and that we should preach, is that the Kingdom of God has come to earth and, through Jesus, we can all become part of it.

7. The degree to which we enjoy our Kingdom citizenship depends upon the degree of our willingness to be bold and claim what is rightfully ours—what Jesus has restored to us through His death and resurrection.

8. The good news is that in Christ we are citizens of the Kingdom of heaven, and all the resources of that Kingdom are available to us to help us live in victory on a daily basis in the here and now.

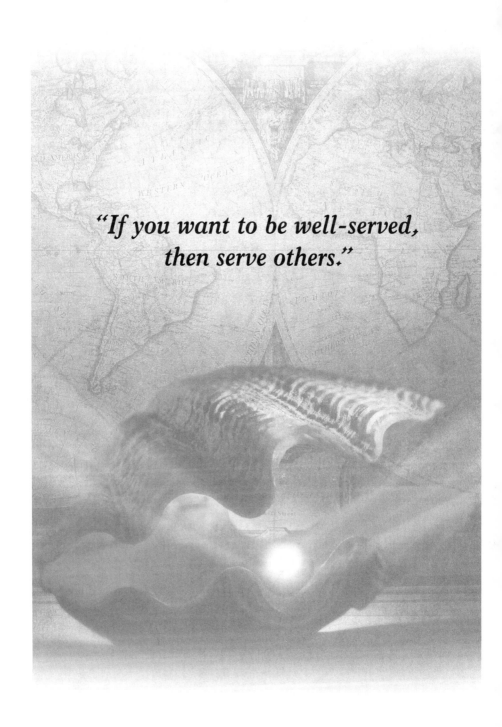

*"If you want to be well-served,
then serve others."*

CHAPTER SIX

A KINGDOM OF SERVANT KINGS

The Kingdom of God is the only Kingdom in which every citizen is designated a king. Their rulership is not over people, but in a specific area of gifting. This is why Jesus is referred to as the King of kings and Lord of lords. We are kings who serve the world with our God-given gift. We serve our way into leadership. This is what Jesus meant when he said, "the greatest among you shall be your servant." The kingdom functions on the basis of servant leadership.

Once we have entered the door, there is nothing more vital to our spiritual growth than to understand the nature of the Kingdom of which we are now citizens. Our hearts should reflect Christ's heart, and our minds, His mind. The Kingdom represents the heart of the entire work of God. Everything God says and does relates to His Kingdom. That is why it is so important that we understand its nature. If we are to be faithful children of the King and ready to rule the dominion He has given us, we must know His heart and how to rule in His name.

Our culture is disintegrating all around us. People are living in despair. All we have to do is read a newspaper or listen to a news broadcast any day of the week to realize that daily life in the world we live in is full of uncertainty and instability. War, hunger, poverty, ignorance, ethnic cleansing, age-old hatreds and prejudices, suicide bombings, terrorism, AIDS and other afflictions, economic instability with wide fluctuations in the stock market—all of these show clearly that our world is a frightening and unreliable place. Because the kingdom of this world is temporary and will one day pass away, it has nothing of enduring quality in which we can trust with any confidence.

Millions die every day from disease, starvation, or violence. The stock market collapses and people who were millionaires one day are paupers the next. Corporations downsize and thousands are suddenly jobless. Extended joblessness creates financial distress resulting in evictions, which increases homelessness and the welfare burden of the state. Religious hatred between Christians, Muslims, and Jews fuels daily conflict in many parts of the world, particularly the Middle East.

A Kingdom That Cannot Be Overthrown

Is there any good news in the midst of all of this? Yes, indeed there is. For those who live and walk in the Kingdom of God, every day can be a good day, regardless of circumstances in the world. No matter how much unrest and turmoil swirls around us in the physical world, the Kingdom of God is stable. It cannot be moved. The governments of this world are shaky and untrustworthy and the global economy is unpredictable. God's government, on the other hand, is firmly established from eternity past and will be in place through eternity future, safe, secure, and unshakable. Unlike the kingdoms of this world, God's Kingdom is founded on eternal principles that will never fade or pass away.

Mankind has tried in so many ways to relieve the fear, pain, and suffering that characterize so much of human life on earth. One way is through religion, which has not been any more successful than anything else because it too is a product of human invention and design. Religion is *man's* attempt to discover God and find the solutions to his own problems.

This is why God did not send us a religion. Instead, He sent us His Kingdom, eternal and unshakable. God's Kingdom came to earth through the person of His Son, Jesus Christ, who was its herald as well as its gateway. Christ did not come to earth to start a religion or a religious organization or club. Jesus preached the Kingdom, but the Church preaches so many other things rather than the Kingdom.

Jesus' mission consisted of five specific goals:

- He came to *reintroduce* the Kingdom of God on earth to man.

- He came to *restore* the righteousness and holiness of mankind.

- He came to *restore* the Holy Spirit in man.

162

- Jesus came to *retrain* mankind for Kingdom leadership.

- He came to *restore* the Kingdom rulership of God on earth through mankind—to *return* administration of God's Kingdom on earth to God's earthly kings.

THE ORIGINAL ORDER OF THE KINGDOM

Jesus' overarching mission on earth was to *reintroduce* the Kingdom of God on earth to mankind. The prefix "re-" means to "do again" or to "go back to the original state." Whenever we "re-" something, we are moving backward. This little two-letter prefix is one of the most important prefixes in the Scriptures, so important, in fact, that I call it the "paradoxical prefix of God." Virtually every word used in the Bible to describe God's program for mankind begins with it. Here are a few of them: redeem, revive, restore, repent, reconcile, resurrection, return, recompense, renew, reward. All of these words relate in one way or another to God's plan for the salvation of man.

When we say that Jesus came to *reintroduce* the Kingdom of God on earth, this implies that at one time it was here before. Christ did not bring a new Kingdom to earth, but an old, original Kingdom that had been lost. At one time, Adam and Eve *were* the Kingdom of God on earth, ruling from the Garden of Eden. When they rebelled against God and fell into sin, the Kingdom departed. How did the Kingdom of God leave?

God's plan had been to rule the earth through a family, called mankind. Adam and Eve's connection to God was the Holy Spirit, who dwelled in them. Their sin corrupted them and made them unholy vessels that were no longer fit to carry the Holy Spirit. The Spirit departed, taking with Him man's only direct connection to God and, therefore, the earth's only direct connection to the Kingdom of God.

Here is how the Kingdom was supposed to work. God the Father and Creator is in heaven, where He has always been. Remember that Jesus taught us to pray, "Our Father *in heaven.*" Heaven is the domain of the Father, a spiritual realm that is invisible, yet greater and more real than the visible, physical realm that was created from it. God is the King of heaven, the Lord of all, the Creator, and the manufacturer of all things.

He is the great Almighty, omnipotent, omniscient, and omnipresent, Elohim, Yahweh, Adonai, El Shaddai—there are so many names and titles that we can ascribe to Him, and still only scratch the surface of all He is.

THE ORIGINS OF MAN

Man the creature is on the earth. Created in God's own image and formed from the dust of the ground, man was placed in administrative authority over the earth and all its other creatures. The Book of Genesis uses several different words for "man" both to designate the human race as a whole and to distinguish between male and female. For instance, in Genesis 1:26, God says, "Let Us make man in Our image, in Our likeness...." In this case the Hebrew word for "man" is *adam*, and refers generically to the entire human race both male and female. It is also used as a proper name for the first man, Adam. The word *adam* literally means "ruddy" or "dark earth," in reference to mankind's original skin color and to the matter from which he was formed.

When the narrative in Genesis turns to the creation of woman, it employs more specific words.

> *Then the Lord God made a woman from the rib He had taken out of the man, and He brought her to the man. The man said, "This is now bone of my bones and flesh of my flesh; she shall be called 'woman,' for she was taken out of man." For this reason a man will leave his father and mother and be united to his wife, and they will become one flesh* (Gen. 2:22-24).

Although verse 23 uses *adam* for "man," verse 24 uses a different word: *ish*, which refers to a man in the individual and specifically male sense. The feminine form of *ish* is *ishshah*, which is used in verses 22 and 23 for "woman," to designate the female "man" as distinct from the male "man." Although *adam* is sometimes used to designate specific individuals (such as Adam, the first man), it is used most often in a generic sense to refer to the human race as a whole. For example, Genesis 5:1-2 says, "This is the written account of Adam's line. When God created man [*adam*], He made him in the likeness of God. He created them male and female and blessed them. And when they were created, He called them 'man' [*adam*]." Therefore, "man" (*adam*) is the general name for the entire human species, both male and female.

THE SPIRITUAL AND THE NATURAL

God created man in His own image. Since God is spirit this means that man was created first as a spirit with the ability to communicate with the spiritual realm. As the breath of God was breathed into man he became a living soul, endowed with self-awareness, personality, and free will. In order to fulfill His design and intention of ruling the earth through a physical representative, God then placed the spirit man He had created into a physical shell, a body fashioned from the dust ("dark earth," or *adam*) of the ground.

So here we have two realms: a spiritual realm capable of touching the realm of God, and a physical realm able to communicate in the earth regions. God's purpose was for man to rule the earth in His name and under His authority. This meant that God's thoughts and desires were to be manifested in the mind of man so that God's will could be done on earth. The only way that God's will can be accomplished on earth without God leaving heaven was for God to get His will into the mind and heart of man. In other words, in order for God to rule the earth through the man He had created, there had to be a spiritual connection linking the two realms. For this reason, God created man with the capacity of receiving His Spirit.

HOLY SPIRIT—GOD'S LINK WITH MAN

The Spirit of God was the vital link between man's dominion on earth and God's dominion in heaven. He revealed the will of God to man and provided wisdom and guidance so that man could carry out God's will on earth. In this original order of things, perfect harmony existed between God and man. There was unity between heaven and earth. Everything operated as it was supposed to. It did not stay that way.

JESUS CAME TO REINTRODUCE THE KINGDOM

Just as God made woman to be a helper and equal partner to the man, so He gave the Holy Spirit to help man (both male and female) administer his earthly domain in accordance with God's will. The Gospel of John refers to the Holy Spirit as a "counselor." Jesus said:

> *And I will ask the Father, and He will give you another Counselor to be with you forever—the Spirit of truth. The world cannot accept*

Him, because it neither sees Him nor knows Him. But you know Him, for He lives with you and will be in you (John 14:16-17).

In Greek, the word for *counselor* is *parakletos*, which also means "advocate" and "comforter." Literally, *parakletos* means "one called alongside." The Holy Spirit's purpose, then as well as now, was to come alongside mankind and help us know and do the Father's will. He does not control us against our will. He convicts us when we do something wrong, guides us along the right path, nudges us to get started doing God's will, and directs our course, but He controls only as much of us as we surrender to Him.

Whatever God wanted, the Holy Spirit revealed to the man and the man manifested it on earth. God wanted His Kingdom rulership to come to earth, but He could only do this through His children who are connected to Him by the Spirit of God.

For to us God revealed them through the Spirit; for the Spirit searches all things, even the depths of God. For who among men knows the thoughts of a man except the spirit of the man which is in him? Even so the thoughts of God no one knows except the Spirit of God. Now we have received, not the spirit of the world, but the Spirit who is from God, that we might know the things freely given to us by God, which things we also speak, not in words taught by human wisdom, but in those taught by the Spirit, combining spiritual thoughts with spiritual words (1 Cor. 2:10-13NAS).

With God's Spirit living inside him and directing his thoughts and life according to God's will, man could manifest God's Kingdom on the earth.

A DISTURBANCE IN THE FORCE

The key to man's being able to manifest the Kingdom of God here on earth is the presence of the Holy Spirit. Man cannot know God's will except through the Holy Spirit living within him, and the Holy Spirit can live only in a holy vessel. Adam and Eve, the first human couple, were filled with the Holy Spirit and enjoyed intimate fellowship with God. When they were seduced and deceived by satan's temptation and disobeyed God, that line of communication was broken, creating a disturbance in the force of the universe. Sin corrupted them. They became unholy vessels, and the Holy Spirit departed, cutting off their connection with the heavenly realm.

Man was still on the earth. He was still a spirit inhabiting a flesh and blood body. He was still designed to dominate the earth, but the earth was now dominating him. Everything was reversed from the original order. Against his will, man found himself enslaved to his unbridled passions, uncontrollable desires, and baser instincts. Man became subject to the very things he was supposed to rule over. Since the Holy Spirit departed, man came under the control of another spirit, an ungodly spirit, lucifer, that unemployed cherub.

Thousands of years passed, during which time God was executing His plan to restore His original order and design. He called Abraham, created a nation from Abraham's descendants, delivered that nation from slavery in Egypt, and brought them into their own land. Within that nation He established a kingly line through David, a line that He promised would reign forever. In the fullness of time Jesus came—in the flesh, a lineal descendant of David born to a virgin named Mary; but in spirit, the Christ, the Son of the living God.

THE HOLY SPIRIT IS BACK

In Jesus Christ, the Holy Spirit returned to earth to dwell in full force in a human being for the first time since leaving Adam and Eve in the Garden of Eden. Christ, the Anointed One, the eternal Son of God, came to earth, born as a human being named Jesus. The man Jesus was flesh, but the Christ within was full of the Spirit. He was Jesus Christ, the God-man, God in the flesh. In Him the fullness of God dwelled in bodily form (see Col. 2:9). That fullness was the Holy Spirit, who was now abiding and dwelling in human flesh for the first time since Eden. Jesus modeled for all mankind the spiritual potential that could belong to them if they were empowered by the Spirit of God.

When Jesus, full of the Holy Spirit, began His public ministry, His message was the simple announcement, *"Repent, for the kingdom of heaven is near"* (Matt. 4:17). His words were addressed to all of us, the entire race of man (*adam*). The word *repent*, as we've already seen, means "to change our mind." Jesus was saying, "Repent, change your mind because your thoughts are corrupt." Why are they corrupt? Because of sin. Why should we change our minds? Because the Kingdom of heaven is near. We need to change our minds because the Kingdom of heaven, absent on earth for centuries, has now returned. Jesus came to reintroduce the Kingdom of heaven on earth. It is here now, and we need to adjust our thinking to that *new* reality.

JESUS CAME TO RESTORE RIGHTEOUSNESS AND HOLINESS TO MANKIND

Not only did Jesus come to reintroduce the Kingdom, but He came also to restore righteousness and holiness to mankind, both of which we lost in the Garden of Eden. Many people have the wrong idea about righteousness. They assume that being righteous means doing right things. For some, it means wearing long dresses or coats and ties, or never smiling or laughing or having any fun. It means wearing crosses around their necks and carrying big Bibles. They proclaim this diluted message by adorning their cars with bumper stickers that say things such as, "Honk if you love Jesus."

That's not righteousness. Righteousness has more to do with a condition of life as opposed to religious actions. Right actions are important, but they should grow out of a person's condition of *being* righteous. Too many people get it backward, believing or assuming that acting right *makes* them righteous. This is not the case. Righteousness is actually a legal term that means to be rightly positioned. A righteous person, then, is someone who is in right standing with the authorities.

When Adam and Eve sinned, they lost the Holy Spirit. They lost their fellowship with God and fell out of right standing with the sole ruling authority of the Kingdom of heaven. The relationship they had once enjoyed with God as their Father was broken. Even though they had been created to dominate the earth, with their connecting link to God's Kingdom severed, they did not know what to do or how to do it. Adam and Eve completely lost sight of their purpose.

In a fallen world, there is no such thing as a "normal" person. God designed us for righteousness and holiness, and without them we are abnormal. We are deficient and defective, unable to function properly in the environment for which we were designed. That is why crime exists.

That is why we as a race hate each other and why we fight and kill each other. Our lack of righteousness and holiness manifests itself in our lives. We destroy each other because we don't know why we are here, and the very environment we were created to rule ends up ruling us.

Jesus restored us to righteousness—to right standing with the Father—through His death for our sins. He made us righteous again, and when He did so, He also restored our holiness. To be holy means to be pure, without spot or blemish, set apart exclusively for God. When Adam and Eve sinned, they showed contempt for their holy state and took that which was meant for God and used it for profane and common purposes. That would be like taking a beautiful, solid gold goblet and using it to hold bacon grease.

How Does One Become Holy?

How does Jesus make us righteous and holy again? Nothing less than the blood of Jesus was required. The Word of God says, "In fact, the law requires that nearly everything be cleansed with blood, and without the shedding of blood there is no forgiveness" (Heb. 9:22). Only the blood of Jesus could cleanse our sin and remove the shame of our actions. That is why He had to die. Just like the old hymn declares, "What can wash away my sin? Nothing but the blood of Jesus." Christ, the Son of God, was Spirit, with no body or blood; Jesus, the man, had both. Jesus Christ was both 100 percent flesh-and-blood man and 100 percent divine Son of God. We cannot separate the two; to do so would be to deny the work that He did on the cross. We cannot worship Christ and forget about Jesus because without Jesus we cannot have Christ. The blood of Jesus cleansed our sin and created the basis for our forgiveness, making it possible for Christ to restore us to righteousness and holiness and bring us the Holy Spirit.

This is why any religion that denies Jesus has a problem. Everything is wrapped up in Jesus Christ and what He did on the cross. If we do not have Jesus, that means our sins are still with us. Without Jesus we do not have His blood to cleanse our sins, and without the cleansing of our sins, we cannot become holy. Unless we become holy, we cannot receive the Holy Spirit. Unless we receive the Holy Spirit, we cannot become citizens of the Kingdom of God.

THE IMPORTANCE OF THE BLOOD OF JESUS

In God's Kingdom economy, blood is absolutely necessary for our restoration. That is why the Jewish law in the Old Testament required blood sacrifices of animals. They were a constant visual reminder that the blood of an innocent victim was the price required to take away our sins. In this way, the Jewish sacrificial system prefigured, or looked ahead to, the day when Jesus, the Lamb of God, pure and sinless, would shed His blood. His blood was sufficient once and for all to cleanse us and to cover our sin.

The first thing God did to deal with Adam and Eve's sin was to cover them with innocent blood: *"The Lord God made garments of skin for Adam and his wife and clothed them"* (Gen. 3:21). God killed an animal of some kind, probably a sheep, ram, or goat, took its bloody skin, and made garments for Adam and Eve to wear. With this act, God revealed to them that the cost of covering their sin was the shed blood of an innocent victim. Only blood can cover sin. Adam and Eve had tried to cover themselves with fig leaves, but that was inadequate because no blood was involved. They were still in their sin.

An animal sacrifice was only a symbol of covered sin; the death of a lamb could never truly take away the sin of man. Only a sacrifice equal in stature to man would qualify. In other words, only the shed blood of a human being would be sufficient to cleanse human sin. Not just any human would do; it had to be a human without any sin of his own, a human who was already pure and spotless and holy. Jesus Christ, the sinless Son of God, born of the Virgin Mary, is the only person who met the requirement. God sent His only begotten Son as a sacrifice to ransom us from sin because no one else could. Christ alone was qualified.

THE KINGDOM IS NOT A RELIGION

The Kingdom is not a religion because religion is man's search for God. With the Kingdom the search is over; God has revealed Himself to man and sent His Son to set us free from our sin and restore us to Himself. The Kingdom is not a religion but a relationship, an intimate communion in which we enter into a deeply personal relationship with the living Christ. Of all the faith systems in the world, the Kingdom alone is effective because it alone has the blood of Christ, which takes away the sin of man. It alone has the Spirit of God dwelling in the lives of believers. It alone can restore us to righteousness and holiness.

The blood of Jesus is critical. No matter how often we go to church, no matter how active we are, no matter how many times we receive communion, no matter how much money we give in the offering, and no matter how much time we spend helping the poor or the sick, unless we have confessed Jesus Christ as our Savior and Lord and allowed His blood to cover and cleanse us, we are still lost and are aliens from the Kingdom. Good works won't cut it. Sound theology won't cut it. Correct doctrine won't cut it. Only the blood of Jesus can cleanse us of sin and make us righteous and holy again. Good works, sound theology, and correct doctrine are byproducts of a growing life in the Spirit. But apart from the blood of Jesus they have no power.

Jesus came to reintroduce the Kingdom of God to mankind and restore us to righteousness and holiness. He accomplished this by dying on the cross, where His shed blood had the power to cover and wash away our sin. Because of our sin, we were spiritually dead, slaves to our sin and hostage to satan and his kingdom of darkness. By His death on the cross, Jesus paid the ransom to free us from satan's grip. He became our substitute so that we could go free. Jesus became sin for us so that we could become the righteousness of God (see 2 Cor. 5:21). His dead body lay in the tomb for three days, cold and lifeless. Death could not hold Him. On the morning of that third day, He rose from the dead. Jesus' resurrection guarantees that all who have been washed clean of sin by His blood will also share in His life—eternal life.

JESUS CAME TO RESTORE THE HOLY SPIRIT IN MAN

The third goal of Jesus' mission on earth was to restore the Holy Spirit in the heart of man. Before this could happen, He had to accomplish the first two goals: to reintroduce the Kingdom, and to restore our righteousness and holiness through His blood. Only when we were clean and holy once again would we be fit vessels for the Holy Spirit's indwelling presence.

Why is the Holy Spirit so important? As we have seen before, He is the link, the spiritual connection between us and the Kingdom of God. He is the one who fills us with spiritual power, guides us, leads us into the knowledge of the truth, and brings to our remembrance all the things that Jesus taught. Jesus promised His disciples that after He left He would send the Holy Spirit to be with them forever.

The Holy Spirit could not come until Jesus had completed His work on the cross, risen from the dead, and applied His blood for the cleansing of man's sin. Once we were cleansed and made holy again, we were ready to receive the Holy Spirit. Jesus took care of that, too, before He ascended into heaven.

> On the evening of that first day of the week, when the disciples were together, with the doors locked for fear of the Jews, Jesus came and stood among them and said, "Peace be with you!" After He said this, He showed them His hands and side. The disciples were overjoyed when they saw the Lord. Again Jesus said, "Peace be with you! As the Father has sent Me, I am sending you." And with that He breathed on them and said, "Receive the Holy Spirit. If you forgive anyone his sins, they are forgiven; if you do not forgive them, they are not forgiven" (John 20:19-23).

In the evening of the very day He rose from the dead, Jesus appeared to His disciples, breathed on them, and imparted the Holy Spirit to them. Later, on the day of Pentecost, they would receive the infilling of the Holy Spirit in power, but here Jesus released the Spirit to them as a continuing indwelling presence. By this act, Jesus returned to mankind that which Adam and Eve had lost in Eden. The link was restored. All who would believe and trust Christ for the forgiveness of their sins and commit their lives to Him would receive the Holy Spirit and thus regain their connection to and citizenship in the Kingdom of God. They could then know the will of God and through them His will could be done on the earth.

TRAINING TO BECOME ROYALTY IN THE HEAVENLY KINGDOM

As children of God, we are part of the royal family of the Kingdom of heaven. Like any other member of royalty, we don't just step into the role without any preparation; we must be trained. Proper and careful training is essential for rulers in the making.

We can see a perfect example of this in the British royal family in the upbringing of Prince William and his younger brother, Prince Harry. Sons of Prince Charles, the future King of England, and the late Princess Diana, the two young men have been groomed from birth for the very special place they occupy as heirs to the throne. From their earliest days, they were taught that they were royalty, even before they were old enough to understand what that meant. Can you imagine trying to tell a two-year-old that he would be king someday? At that age, he doesn't care; he's too busy smearing peanut butter on his face. Nevertheless, even at such a young age, it is important for a prince to be told who he is. No age is too young to begin learning self-identity.

As the older of the two, Prince William stands second in line to the throne of England, after his father, Prince Charles. Even before Prince William was born, while his mother, Princess Diana, was in the delivery room, a group of tutors were on hand to begin their work. Although each one had a different specific responsibility, their overall task was the same: to teach the young prince who he was and train him how to act accordingly. There is a certain posture, deportment, behavior, and manner of speech expected of royalty, and it does not develop automatically. From the day they were born, Princes William and Harry were taught how to walk, talk, think, and behave like kings.

In the same way, we must learn how to think and act like the royal children of the heavenly King. We have spent so long in the condition and mentality of slaves in the kingdom of darkness that we automatically think and act like slaves. If we are to exercise our full status and potential in the earthly realm as ambassadors of our Father, we must be retrained in the behavior and mindset of the Kingdom. In this task, the Holy Spirit is our tutor.

The day Prince William came home from the hospital he was placed in the primary care of those responsible for his princely training. Princess Diana certainly had regular access to her son, but his day-to-day training as a royal was in the hands of his tutors. Royalty walks a certain way, so Prince William was taught how to walk like a king. Royalty sits a certain way, so he was taught how to sit like a king. Royalty speaks a certain way, so he was taught how to speak like a king. His diction, tone of voice, and manner of speaking were all carefully nurtured and polished.

He was taught not to raise his voice, because royalty never has to shout. The power of a king's voice is not in its volume but in its authority of position.

When we first become believers, we receive our new spiritual birth from Jesus Christ, who then "turns us over," in a manner of speaking, to someone else—the Holy Spirit—for our training and upbringing as children of the King. Our faith is based on a personal relationship with Jesus Christ, but since He is in heaven seated at the right hand of the Father, the way He relates to us and we to Him is through the Holy Spirit. In His earthly incarnation, Jesus could not be continuously and physically present with all His followers, so He promised to send His Spirit who would abide with us forever and teach us how to think and act like the royalty we are:

> *And I will ask the Father, and He will give you another Counselor to be with you forever—the Spirit of truth....But the Counselor, the Holy Spirit, whom the Father will send in My name, will teach you all things and will remind you of everything I have said to you* (John 14:16-17,26).

> *But I tell you the truth: It is for your good that I am going away. Unless I go away, the Counselor will not come to you; but if I go, I will send Him to you....But when He, the Spirit of truth, comes, He will guide you into all truth. He will not speak on His own; He will speak only what He hears, and He will tell you what is yet to come* (John 16:7-7,13).

THE HOLY SPIRIT IS OUR PERSONAL TUTOR

We need a tutor like the Holy Spirit because our minds and thinking are corrupt and it takes us a while to grasp and genuinely believe the truth about who we are in Christ. We are royal children of the Kingdom of God, but have spent our entire lives living in the slave quarters. Our thoughts and behavior won't change overnight. The Holy Spirit lives in us as a continuing abiding presence, patiently and lovingly teaching us who we are and how to think, speak, and act accordingly.

Royals such as Princes William and Harry are taught how to walk, talk, sit, stand, and eat in a manner consistent with who they are. Their every action, gesture, and mannerism is designed to display authority. This was evident even at their mother's funeral. After Princess Diana died so tragically, her sons Prince William and Prince Harry, even as they stood weeping and mourning her death, nevertheless comported themselves as royalty, just as they had been taught. Even in the midst of their tears, they never dropped their aura of authority.

One of the things the Holy Spirit teaches us is how to stand in authority as true sons and daughters of God no matter what troubles or difficulties come into our lives. As royal children of our heavenly Father, we can take charge of our circumstances, rather than being a slave to them. We can live daily in power and victory, rather than in weakness and defeat. All it takes is training, and the Holy Spirit is our Teacher.

Jesus Came to Retrain Mankind for Kingdom Leadership

The fourth goal of Jesus' mission on earth was to retrain mankind for Kingdom leadership. He came to teach us how to think and act like God once again. Jesus replicated the message that He proclaimed and by the power of the Spirit we are also empowered to model and preach the message of the Kingdom. Jesus established the standard by the example of His own life. In every word, action, and moment of His life on earth, Jesus showed us what the Father is like and what we should be like as His children. Like us, Jesus' disciples did not always understand this easily:

Thomas said to Him, "Lord, we don't know where You are going, so how can we know the way?" Jesus answered, "I am the way and the truth and the life. No one comes to the Father except through Me. If you really knew Me, you would know My Father as well. From now on, you do know Him and have seen Him." Philip said "Lord, show us the Father and that will be enough for us." Jesus answered: "Don't you know Me, Philip, even after I have been among you such a long time? Anyone who has seen Me has seen the Father. How can you say, 'Show us the Father'? Don't you believe that I am in the Father, and that the Father is in Me? The words I say to you are not just My own. Rather, it is the Father, living in Me, who is doing His work" (John 14:5-10).

Retraining us to think and act like children of the King was perhaps the toughest part of Jesus' mission because we tend to be so stubborn, hardheaded, and slow to learn. This is due, in part, to our blindness and spiritual dullness because of our sin and, in part, to the fact that we as a race of people have been separated from God's royal and holy environment for so long. God created us in His own image as His royal sons and daughters, and designed us to rule the earthly realm as He ruled the heavenly realm. Our sin evicted us from the place we were destined to fill, and for millennia we have been like the prodigal son of Luke 15:11-32, living in the pigpen and feeding on the same corn husks that the pigs eat. We have been out of touch with "home" for so long that we have lost sight, not only of our identity, but also of our destiny. Jesus came to lead us to rediscover both and to retrain us in how to reclaim and live in them.

Jesus accomplished this for us by giving us a perfect model of the Father. As mentioned previously, if we want to know what God the Father is like, all we have to do is look at Jesus. If we want to know what we should be like as children of the Father, all we have to do is look at Jesus, who is the only begotten Son of the Father. The Holy Spirit in us enables us to understand what we see in Jesus and what we hear in His teachings, and gives us the power to carry them over into our lives.

HEALING THE MENTAL DAMAGE CAUSED BY THE GREAT FALL

In the kingdom of darkness we have been under satan's sway. Kicked out of heaven for rebelling against God, satan fell to earth as a nobody, then pretended to be a somebody by tricking Adam and Eve and usurping their earthly authority. Ever since then he has taught mankind to think of themselves as nobodies, just as he is. After a lifetime of feeding on negativity and impossibility thinking, most of us have a certain amount of mental damage that the Holy Spirit must heal. We have been slaves for so long that we don't know how to handle freedom. We apologize for getting ahead. We don't believe we deserve or are entitled to the best. That may have been true while we were sinners lost and separated from God. As believers, however, we have been restored to our place as God's children and are entitled to all the blessings and benefits of that station.

The retraining of our minds is part of what it means to give ourselves as living sacrifices to God. We cannot live effectively for the Lord until we learn to think like Him. That is what the apostle Paul meant when he wrote to the Roman believers,

> *Therefore, I urge you, brothers, in view of God's mercy, to offer your bodies as living sacrifices, holy and pleasing to God—this is your spiritual act of worship. Do not conform any longer to the pattern of this world, but be transformed by the renewing of your mind. Then you will be able to test and approve what God's will is—His good, pleasing and perfect will* (Rom. 12:1-2).

Paul is saying that we should not allow ourselves any longer to be molded by the world we have lived in all our lives but to be transformed by renewing our minds to think and conform to the mind of Christ. Renewing our minds means returning to the original mind that we had before the fall, a mind that loves and honors God and that understands its rightful place as a vice-regent of the earthly domain under God's sovereign Kingdom rule.

JESUS CAME TO RESTORE KINGDOM RULERSHIP ON EARTH

Lastly, Jesus' mission on earth was to restore the Kingdom rulership of God on earth through mankind. Once again, His own life was an example of the Kingdom on earth in action. Whenever Jesus healed the sick, raised the dead, walked on water, calmed a storm with a word, or fed a multitude with a handful of fish and bread, He demonstrated the truth that God's Kingdom had come to earth. Whenever He preached the good news of the Kingdom, or taught His followers about life in that Kingdom, and whenever people responded to Him in faith, He demonstrated the power of the Kingdom to impact human life and environment.

Despite Adam and Eve's fall in the Garden of Eden, God's desire never changed. He still wanted to rule the earth by manifesting His Kingdom through the Holy Spirit in the lives of people who were committed to Him and sold out to His lordship. For 2,000 years, ever since the days of Jesus, He has been doing this in increasing degree as men, women, and children in every generation have given their lives to Christ and allowed the Holy Spirit to work in and through them.

YOUR PLACE IN THE KINGDOM

Each of us who turn to Christ becomes a "stone" in the magnificent spiritual "palace" of the Kingdom of God on earth, called and equipped as kings and priests to represent that Kingdom before the rest of the world. The apostle Peter stated it this way:

As you come to Him, the living Stone—rejected by men but chosen by God and precious to Him—you also, like living stones, are being built into a spiritual house to be a holy priesthood, offering spiritual sacrifices acceptable to God through Jesus Christ. For in Scripture it says: "See, I lay a stone in Zion, a chosen and precious cornerstone, and the one who trusts in Him will never be put to shame."...But you are a chosen people, a royal priesthood, a holy nation, a people belonging to God, that you may declare the praises of Him who called you out of darkness into His wonderful light. Once you were not a people, but now you are the people of God; once you had not received mercy, but now you have received mercy (1 Pet. 2:4-6;9-10).

Throughout human history, the religious society has generally separated priest and king into separate offices and functions, but God did not design them that way in the beginning. When God created us, He intended for us to be His representative rulers—His ambassadors—over the rest of the created order. We were to be priest/kings in the earth: as priests, representing God's nature and character, and as kings, His Kingdom government.

Through Christ we are a "holy priesthood," a "chosen people," a "royal priesthood," and a "holy nation." As such, we have been restored to our priestly function of representing and reflecting God's nature and character before the world. We are also the "people of God," not a nation of subjects, but of sons and daughters. If God is a King, then we, His people, are also of the royal line. Therefore, we have also been restored to our kingly function of representing the government of God on the earth.

God is not interested in having subjects in His Kingdom. He wants only children, royal heirs to the treasures of His domain. Our mission as ambassadors of the Kingdom of God is to bring those who are enslaved in the kingdom of darkness to Christ, the door, so that He can set them free to enter into their full citizenship in God's Kingdom of light.

PRINCIPLES

1. God's Kingdom is founded on eternal principles that will never fade or pass away.

2. Jesus' overarching mission on earth was to *reintroduce* the Kingdom of God on earth to mankind.

3. The key to man's manifesting the Kingdom of God here on earth is the presence of the Holy Spirit.

4. Jesus came to restore righteousness and holiness to man.

5. In God's Kingdom economy, blood is absolutely necessary for our restoration.

6. Jesus came to restore the Holy Spirit in mankind.

7. If we are to exercise our full status and potential in the earthly realm as ambassadors of our Father, we must be retrained in the behavior and mindset of the Kingdom.

8. As royal children of our heavenly Father, we can take charge of our circumstances rather than being a slave to them.

9. Jesus came to retrain mankind for Kingdom leadership.

10. Jesus came to restore the Kingdom rulership of God on earth through mankind.

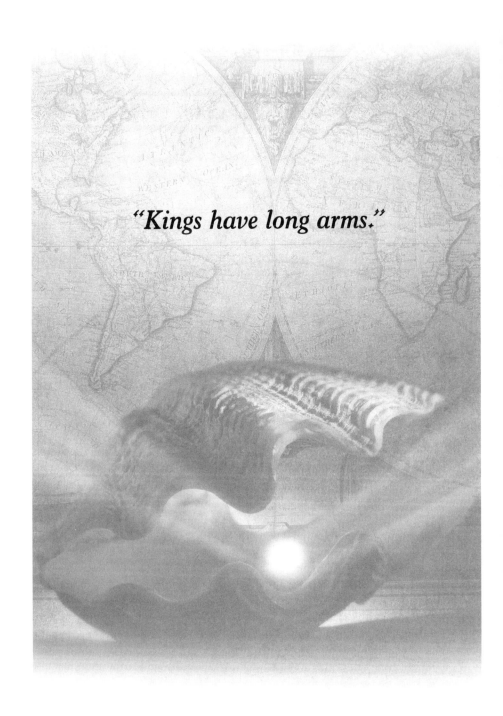

"Kings have long arms."

KINGS, PROPHETS, AND THE KINGDOM

Normally, when we talk about the Kingdom of God, we think only of what Jesus said about the subject as recorded in the four Gospels. Although it is certainly true that in His life and words Jesus revealed the Kingdom more fully than ever before, they were simply the culmination of all that God had been working toward from the beginning, as was His life in general. Everything God says and does relates to His Kingdom. The entire Bible deals with the Kingdom of God. From Genesis to Revelation, Scripture reveals God as the great and almighty King of heaven and earth resolutely at work on His plan of the ages.

> *"And you shall be to Me a kingdom of priests and a holy nation."*
> *These are the words that you shall speak to the sons of Israel*
> (Exod. 19:6, NAS).

> *For the kingdom is the Lord's, and He rules over the nations* (Ps. 22:28, NAS).

> *Your throne, O God, is forever and ever; a scepter of uprightness is the scepter of Your kingdom* (Psalm 45:6).

> *They shall speak of the glory of Your kingdom, and talk of Your power* (Ps. 145:11, NAS).

> *And in the days of those kings the God of heaven will set up a kingdom which will never be destroyed, and that kingdom will not be left for another people; it will crush and put an end to all these kingdoms, but it will itself endure forever* (Dan. 2:44, NAS).

That plan is to reverse and destroy the works of the devil and fully restore His rule over the earthly realm through His human representatives.

We have already said that the Bible is not about religion, but about a Kingdom. Everything centers on the Kingdom of God. All the saints of the Old Testament recognized this fact. Abraham knew it. Moses knew it. Samuel knew it. David, the king of Israel, knew it. The prophets knew it. Jesus knew it. All the apostles and other believers in the New Testament knew it. Everyone, it seems, understood the priority of the Kingdom; everyone except us, that is. In recent years the focus in much of the Body of Christ has shifted away from the Kingdom of God to other issues. The tragic result is that multitudes of believers today know little about the Kingdom, and even fewer understand their place and rights as its citizens.

Often, even in spite of all our sophistication, education, and technology, we of modern and "enlightened" democratic societies are worse off than the people of Old Testament times when it comes to matters of understanding the Kingdom of God and how our world relates to it.

A King Speaks About the Kingdom

The Book of Psalms is full of references that make it clear that David and other psalm writers in Israel knew and revered God as King of kings:

> *"I have installed My King on Zion, My holy hill." I will proclaim the decree of the Lord: He said to me, "You are My Son; today I have become your Father. Ask of Me, and I will make the nations your inheritance, the ends of the earth your possession. You will rule them with an iron scepter; you will dash them to pieces like pottery"* (Ps. 2:6-9).

Not only do these verses speak of God as King, but they also look ahead prophetically to the coming of Jesus, who would inherit the Kingdom from His Father.

> *The Lord is King for ever and ever; the nations will perish from His land* (Psalm 10:16).

King David understood that human kingdoms are temporary, but God's Kingdom is eternal.

> *Lift up your heads, O you gates; be lifted up, you ancient doors, that the King of glory may come in. Who is this King of glory? The Lord*

strong and mighty, the Lord mighty in battle. Lift up your heads, O you gates; lift them up, you ancient doors, that the King of glory may come in. Who is He, this King of glory? The Lord Almighty— He is the King of glory (Ps. 24:7-10).

The Lord sits enthroned over the flood; the Lord is enthroned as King forever (Ps. 29:10).

In these verses, David, Israel's second and greatest king, praised and acknowledged the Lord God as the "King of glory" who was enthroned forever. The word *glory* literally means "heavy" or "weighty," especially in the sense of referring to someone of great importance and high esteem. With the phrase "King of glory," David exalts God as the greatest King of all and worthy of the highest esteem.

Your throne, O God, will last for ever and ever; a scepter of justice will be the scepter of Your Kingdom (Ps. 45:6).

How awesome is the Lord Most High, the great King over all the earth!...Sing praises to God, sing praises; sing praises to our King, sing praises. For God is the King of all the earth; sing to Him a psalm of praise. God reigns over the nations; God is seated on His holy throne (Ps. 47:2;6-8).

These verses from Psalms (attributed to the "sons of Korah") speak of the throne of God, from where He "reigns over the nations" and extends a "scepter of justice." A scepter is a symbol of kingly rule and authority. Many earthly kings have raised over their subjects a scepter of cruelty and oppression. God's scepter, however—the defining characteristic of His rule—is justice.

The Lord has established His throne in heaven, and His kingdom rules over all (Ps. 103:19).

All You have made will praise You, O Lord; Your saints will extol You. They will tell of the glory of Your kingdom and speak of Your might, so that all men may know of Your mighty acts and the glorious splendor of Your kingdom. Your kingdom is an everlasting kingdom, and Your dominion endures through all generations (Ps. 145:10-13).

David, once again, was focused on the Kingdom of God. Although he himself was a king, David knew his place. More than King Saul who preceded him, and all the other kings who succeeded him, David understood his role not only as a king under God with civic obligations to his people, but also as a priest before God with spiritual responsibilities on behalf of his people. He is an example to all of us of our place in the Kingdom. Like David we are called to rule as kings in this world as well as to fulfill the priestly role of carrying out our spiritual care of the people in the earthly regions.

Ancient Prophets and the Kingdom of God

Psalmists such as David and the sons of Korah were not the only people of Old Testament times who understood the kingship of God and how the kingdoms of men are related to it. Many of the prophets also received powerful visions and insight into the glory and splendor of God and His Kingdom. One of the most familiar of these visions is found in Isaiah:

> *In the year that King Uzziah died, I saw the Lord seated on a throne, high and exalted, and the train of His robe filled the temple. Above Him were seraphs, each with six wings: With two wings they covered their faces, with two they covered their feet, and with two they were flying. And they were calling to one another: "Holy, holy, holy is the Lord Almighty; the whole earth is full of His glory." At the sound of their voices the doorposts and thresholds shook and the temple was filled with smoke. "Woe to me!" I cried. "I am ruined! For I am a man of unclean lips, and I live among a people of unclean lips, and my eyes have seen the King, the Lord Almighty"* (Isa. 6:1-5).

It would be difficult to find a more powerful depiction of a king on his throne than Isaiah's picture of the Lord surrounded by a host of angelic attendants who were ceaselessly praising Him and hastening to do His bidding. Isaiah recognized immediately that he was in the presence of absolute holiness and glory. He had "seen the King, the Lord Almighty," and the majesty of his vision so overwhelmed him that he feared for his life. His own human sinfulness stood out suddenly in such starkness against the awesome purity and holiness of God that Isaiah expected to be struck down any moment.

Instead, he experienced the merciful justice of God:

Then one of the seraphs flew to me with a live coal in his hand, which he had taken with tongs from the altar. With it he touched my mouth and said, "See, this has touched your lips; your guilt is taken away and your sin atoned for." Then I heard the voice of the Lord saying, "Whom shall I send? And who will go for Us?" And I said, "Here am I. Send me!" (Isa. 6:6-8)

Isaiah's vision of God the King precipitated a spiritual crisis in his life. Once he had experienced the cleansing of his sin, the power of his vision inspired him to respond to the King's call. Isaiah became an ambassador for the Lord Almighty, called and appointed to proclaim the message of the Kingdom of God to a wayward people who had ignored and rejected it.

In another place, Isaiah recorded the insight he had received regarding the King's heir and the nature and character of His Kingdom:

For to us a child is born, to us a son is given, and the government will be on His shoulders. And He will be called Wonderful Counselor, Mighty God, Everlasting Father, Prince of Peace. Of the increase of His government and peace there will be no end. He will reign on David's throne and over his kingdom, establishing and upholding it with justice and righteousness from that time on and forever. The zeal of the Lord Almighty will accomplish this (Isa. 9:6-7).

What is the Kingdom of God like? *It is a realm ruled by a God who is mighty and everlasting, and who is a Wonderful Counselor (a wise and just Judge); a realm characterized by peace, justice, and righteousness.*

Jeremiah was another prophet who had a profound understanding of the kingly nature and lofty status of God. He said:

No one is like You, O Lord; You are great, and Your name is mighty in power. Who should not revere You, O King of the nations? This is Your due. Among all the wise men of the nations and in all their kingdoms, there is no one like You. ....But the Lord is the true God; He is the living God, the eternal King. When He is angry, the earth trembles; the nations cannot endure His wrath (Jer. 10:6-7,10).

185

To Jeremiah God was "King of the nations," "the true God...the living God, the eternal King" whom people of all the nations should revere and honor. As King, God sat rightfully as Judge of the earth, and under His wrath and anger the nations could not endure. What a powerful picture of God! Jeremiah knew God as a King who was truly sovereign over His entire domain, both spiritual and physical. The strongest and most fearsome of human kingdoms are nothing in comparison to the Kingdom of God.

A KINGDOM MADE NOT BY HUMAN HANDS

Perhaps no one in the Old Testament received more revelation and insight about God's Kingdom than did the prophet Daniel. As a matter of fact, the entire focus of the Book of Daniel involves the sovereignty of the Kingdom of God over the kingdoms of men. Several times throughout the book, the strength and will of earthly kings are pitted against the strength and will of God, and God comes out on top every time. Nebuchadnezzar's fiery furnace could not touch the servants of God who were covered by His mighty hand, and so Shadrach, Meshach, and Abednego stepped out of the flames without even the smell of smoke on their clothes. A den of hungry lions was no match for the angel of God who shut their mouths and protected Daniel from becoming their next meal.

Daniel was a member of the "exile generation," those Jews who either were removed from their homeland by the Babylonians and forcibly relocated, or who were born in exile in Babylon. Even as a foreigner and an exile, Daniel rose to a position of great prominence and trust as a civic leader and administrator in the Babylonian government. He was a really sharp guy, a true intellectual, superbly educated, and highly gifted as an administrator. In addition to these qualities, Daniel was a man of impeccable integrity who loved God. Because of his extraordinary gifts and competence, Daniel directly served a succession of several Babylonian kings. These rulers wanted trustworthy men around them and could have found no one better than Daniel.

DANIEL AND A KING'S DREAM

Among Daniel's gifts was the God-given ability to interpret dreams, which he did on several occasions. In one instance King Nebuchadnezzar had a puzzling and disturbing dream he could not understand. Summoning the chief magicians, enchanters, sorcerers, and astrologers in his kingdom, he demanded on pain of death that first they tell him what he had dreamed, and then interpret it for him. When they explained that no one could tell him his dream, the king ordered the execution of all the wise men of Babylon. Before the king's decree could be carried out, however, Daniel heard of it and offered both to describe the king's dream and give its interpretation.

When summoned before the king, Daniel correctly explained the dream in every detail. Nebuchadnezzar had seen a great statue with a head of gold, chest and arms of silver, abdomen and thighs of bronze, legs of iron, and feet made partly of iron and partly of clay. Then a stone cut out with no human hand smashed the feet of iron and clay and proceeded to break the rest of the statue into tiny pieces, which the wind blew away. After this, the stone grew into a great mountain that filled the whole earth (see Dan. 2:31-35).

After describing the king's dream, Daniel began his interpretation. He explained that the different parts of the statue represented different kingdoms that would arise in the earth. Nebuchadnezzar's kingdom of Babylon was the head of gold. Then Daniel said:

> After you, another kingdom will rise, inferior to yours. Next, a third kingdom, one of bronze, will rule over the whole earth. Finally, there will be a fourth kingdom, strong as iron—for iron breaks and smashes everything—and as iron breaks things to pieces, so it will crush and break all the others. Just as you saw that the feet and toes were partly of baked clay and partly of iron, so this will be a divided kingdom; yet it will have some of the strength of iron in it, even as you saw iron mixed with clay. As the toes were partly iron and partly clay, so this kingdom will be partly strong and partly brittle. And just as you saw the iron mixed with baked clay, so the people will be a mixture and will not remain united, any more than iron mixes with clay. In the time of those kings, the God of heaven will set up a kingdom that will never be destroyed, nor will it be left to another people. It will crush all those kingdoms and bring them to an end, but it will itself endure forever. This is the meaning of the vision of the rock cut out of a mountain, but not by human hands—a rock that broke the iron, the

bronze, the clay, the silver and the gold to pieces. The great God has shown the king what will take place in the future. The dream is true and the interpretation is trustworthy (Dan. 2:39-45).

Biblical scholars generally agree that except for the feet of iron mixed with clay, the various segments of the statue refer to kingdoms and empires that have come and gone on the earth. Babylon, the golden head, gave way to the Persian Empire, represented by the chest and arms of silver. Persia, in turn, fell to the empire of the Greeks, symbolized by the abdomen and thighs of bronze. The legs of iron stand for the Roman Empire, which was stronger, and more widespread than the Greeks or any other empire that had preceded it. For centuries the Romans crushed all opposition, established a stable government based on law, and became the greatest empire the world had ever known.

The final kingdom, represented by the feet of iron and clay, has not yet appeared on history's stage, but many people believe it is already in the making. Clay and iron do not mix; they cannot be joined together to form a strong and stable mixture. This image, then, refers to an empire or federation that cannot hold together. Many people believe it is a prophecy concerning Europe and, in particular, the modern European Union of our day. The nations of Europe have always struggled to coexist with each other, alternating between devastating war and uneasy peace. According to the Book of Revelation, it is from this governmental system that the "beast" and the antichrist will arise. Some interpret prophecy to say that before Christ returns there will be a resurgence of the Roman Empire, and that the European Union represents this in the process of fulfillment.

THE FINAL KINGDOM

Nevertheless, this future succession of earthly kingdoms is not the focal point of Daniel's interpretation of the king's dream. Another kingdom is coming, symbolized by the stone, a kingdom that will smash and blow away all the others, a kingdom that will grow to fill the whole earth and will last forever. What is this kingdom that Daniel foresaw with prophetic vision? This final and eternal kingdom, this kingdom of the "rock," is the Kingdom of God that would be ushered in by the coming of Christ and would eventually rule absolute and unopposed.

When Jesus came, He spoke of the rock. One day He asked His disciples, *"Who do people say the Son of Man is?"* (Matt. 16:13). After their reply, He got more personal:

> *"But what about you?" He asked. "Who do you say I am?" Simon Peter answered, "You are the Christ, the Son of the living God." Jesus replied, "Blessed are you, Simon son of Jonah, for this was not revealed to you by man, but by my Father in heaven. And I tell you that you are Peter, and on this rock I will build My church, and the gates of Hades will not overcome it" (Matt. 16:15-18).*

Jesus was using a play on words here. The name *Peter*, or *petros* in Greek, means "stone" as in a small rock. When Jesus said "rock," however, He used the word *petra*, which refers to a large boulder. Jesus Himself was the "rock" upon which His Church would be built. He Himself was the rock in Nebuchadnezzar's dream that crushed all the kingdoms of the earth to dust. His is the Kingdom made without human hands that will last forever.

THE CHARACTER OF THE KINGDOM

Chapter seven of the Book of Daniel relates a dream and vision that came to Daniel himself that reveals the character and awesome majesty of the Kingdom of God. Daniel saw a procession of four frightening beasts rising from the sea. The first was "like a lion" with "wings of an eagle." The wings were stripped off, and the beast stood on two feet and was given the "heart of a man" (see Dan. 7:4). Next came a creature that looked like a bear. Following this was a beast that looked like a leopard, except that it had four heads and four wings like birds' wings on its back. The fourth beast was the most terrifying of all, with huge iron teeth that "crushed and devoured its victims," and ten horns. As Daniel watched, three of the horns were uprooted and replaced by one smaller horn, which "had eyes like the eyes of a man and a mouth that spoke boastfully" (Dan. 7:8).

These four beasts, and the fourth one in particular, represent the demonic and satanic forces that lie behind the power, wickedness, and corruption of many kingdoms of the world. As terrifying as these creatures appear to be, the next scene in Daniel's dream puts them in their proper perspective. What follows assures us of both the certain defeat of satan and the absolute triumph of the Kingdom of God.

As I looked, thrones were set in place, and the Ancient of Days took His seat. His clothing was as white as snow; the hair of His head was white like wool. His throne was flaming with fire, and its wheels were all ablaze. A river of fire was flowing, coming out from before Him. Thousands upon thousands attended Him; ten thousand times ten thousand stood before Him. The court was seated, and the books were opened. Then I continued to watch because of the boastful words the horn was speaking. I kept looking until the beast was slain and its body destroyed and thrown into the blazing fire. (The other beasts had been stripped of their authority, but were allowed to live for a period of time.) In my vision at night I looked, and there before me was one like a son of man, coming with the clouds of heaven. He approached the Ancient of Days and was led into His presence. He was given authority, glory and sovereign power; all peoples, nations and men of every language worshiped Him. His dominion is an ever-lasting dominion that will not pass away, and His kingdom is one that will never be destroyed (Dan. 7:9-14).

A Peek Into the Heavenly Realm

What an awesome scene this is, revealing the King of heaven in all His glory, splendor, and majesty. Daniel taxed his vocabulary trying to find words to describe the indescribable. The "Ancient of Days" in verses 9 and 13 is a reference to God the Father, eternal, without beginning or end. His white clothing speaks of His purity and holiness, while the white of His hair suggests the wisdom of the ages. Blazing flames and the river of fire also symbolize God's purity and holiness, as well as His majesty and power.

The Ancient of Days took His seat in the midst of thrones—thousands of them. Thrones are for rulers, and these thrones were the seats of authority for the kingly citizens of the Kingdom, the King's court. Daniel saw many kings, but then the King of kings entered, and all the focus was on Him. Thousands attended Him, as befitted such a great King. These verses at least imply that those who occupied the thrones around the King were also among those who attended Him. Here was a scene unlike anything ever found on earth: kings attending the King; rulers taking care of the Ruler. Earthly kings have servants and advisors attending them. The King of kings, the Ancient of Days, has kings as His attendants.

After the Ancient of Days took His place, the court was seated (no one sits while the King is standing) and the books were opened. This is a scene of judgment, not the judgment of men, but of satan. Daniel saw this in a vision 500 years prior to the birth of Jesus. Satan was judged, his power destroyed, and his body "thrown into the blazing fire." Fire consumes, and here it symbolizes loss of power. The other beasts were also stripped of their authority, but allowed to live for a while.

THE FINAL DESTRUCTION AND THE SON OF MAN

What this means for us is that, even though satan and the forces of darkness are still around to harass us if we let them, their power and authority over us have been broken. They have already been judged. Their final destruction awaits the consummation of all things with the return of Christ, but it is as certain as though it had already happened. This is why we do not have to surrender to defeat or despair or helplessness in our daily lives. We can live in victory and walk in confidence because the power of our enemy has been broken. The Lord has given us authority over him. We are among those seated in judgment over him with the King.

Immediately after this in Daniel's dream, the reason for satan's destruction becomes clear. "One like a son of man, coming with the clouds of heaven" approaches the Ancient of Days and is led into His presence. This is a direct reference to Jesus, 500 years before He was born. Jesus' preferred title for Himself was the "Son of Man." Through His death on the cross and resurrection from the dead, Jesus the Son of Man conquered satan and broke his power and authority forever. With this victory He entered heaven triumphantly where He was given "authority, glory and sovereign power," was worshiped by people of all nations, and ruled "an everlasting dominion," a Kingdom that will never be destroyed. This picture is very similar to Paul's words about Jesus in Philippians:

And being found in appearance as a man, He humbled Himself and became obedient to death—even death on a cross! Therefore God exalted Him to the highest place and gave Him the name that is above every name, that at the name of Jesus every knee should bow, in Heaven and on earth and under the earth, and every tongue confess that Jesus Christ is Lord, to the glory of God the Father (Philippians 2:8-11).

THE SAINTS GET THE KINGDOM

It would be perfectly understandable if Daniel was almost overwhelmed by what he saw in his vision. If I had seen what he saw, I know I would have been. I think most of us would. Indeed, Daniel was deeply affected by his vision, not just the sheer power and majesty of the images themselves, but also by the mystery surrounding them. Daniel longed to know what they meant.

> *I, Daniel, was troubled in spirit, and the visions that passed through my mind disturbed me. I approached one of those standing there and asked him the true meaning of all this. So he told me and gave me the interpretation of these things: "The four great beasts are four kingdoms that will rise from the earth. But the saints of the Most High will receive the kingdom and will possess it forever—yes, for ever and ever" (Dan. 7:15-18).*

Although the four beasts represented four human kingdoms that were to arise, that is not the most important point. What's important is the promise in verse 18 that the saints—the children of God—will receive and possess His Kingdom forever, infinitely longer than the tenure of worldly kingdoms, no matter how great and powerful they may appear.

Daniel then wanted to know the meaning of the fourth and most terrible beast, as well as the meaning behind the ten horns on its head, and the one horn with eyes and a mouth that replaced three of the original ten.

> *As I watched, this horn was waging war against the saints and defeating them, until the Ancient of Days came and pronounced judgment in favor of the saints of the Most High, and the time came when they possessed the Kingdom. He gave me this explanation: "The fourth beast is a fourth kingdom that will appear on earth. It will be different from all the other kingdoms and will devour the whole earth, trampling it down and crushing it. The ten horns are ten kings who will come from this kingdom. After them another king will arise, different from the earlier ones; he will subdue three kings. He will speak against the Most High and oppress His saints and try to*

change the set times and the laws. The saints will be handed over to him for a time, times and half a time. But the court will sit, and his power will be taken away and completely destroyed forever. Then the sovereignty, power and greatness of the kingdoms under the whole heaven will be handed over to the saints, the people of the Most High. His kingdom will be an everlasting kingdom, and all rulers will worship and obey Him." This is the end of the matter. I, Daniel, was deeply troubled by my thoughts, and my face turned pale, but I kept the matter to myself (Dan. 7:21-28).

MAN FORFEITS THE KINGDOM

What did we (the human race) lose at the fall—heaven? No. We did not come from heaven, nor were we created for heaven. We were created from the dust of the earth to rule over the earth. What we lost at the fall was not heaven, but the Kingdom. Jesus died on the cross and rose from the dead not so much to take us to heaven as to bring us back into possession of the Kingdom we lost. When we receive it, we will possess it forever and ever.

Satan will fight against our restoration and his loss of power with everything he's got. This is the conflict that lies behind the rise and activities of the fourth beast. This fourth kingdom probably represents both the Roman Empire as well as the future kingdom of the antichrist. As before, however, the focus of this passage is not on the oppressive power and cruelty of this beast, but on his certain and complete destruction, and the coming of the saints into the eternal Kingdom. These are the very saints whom the beast had persecuted and oppressed.

Verse 27 mentions three specific things that the children of God will receive when they come into the Kingdom:

- Sovereignty;
- Power; and,
- Greatness.

Sovereignty means absolute authority. In a true monarchy, a king is sovereign because his word is law. God is the only *true* Sovereign because He is answerable to no one except Himself. All other sovereignty is delegated sovereignty, which implies a delegator who is greater. Within the scope of our delegated sovereignty, we have absolute authority.

This means that we do not have to sit by helplessly while the enemy wreaks havoc in our lives. We can stand up to him and in the name of Jesus take authority over the situation. That is our right as Kingdom citizens in good standing. Many times we bow under burdens we should not have to bear. Jesus bore our burdens on the cross and bought our victory. Our problem is that we refuse to claim it. Our slave mentality blocks us off from so much that is ours for the asking, and we settle for the far off dream of "pie in the sky by and by."

When Jesus restored the Kingdom to us, He did not give us a pretty façade with nothing inside. Along with the Kingdom He gave us *power*: power to overcome, prosper, live in victory, be joyful, and to fulfill our potential.

Finally, with the Kingdom comes *greatness*. Man was created in God's image, the crowning glory of His creative activity, designed to rule over the earthly domain. As lost and fallen sinners, we still bear God's image, but only a faint shadow of our former glory. When we are restored to the Kingdom, we are restored to greatness, because we return to the place and environment for which we were created.

Jesus said that the key to true greatness is humility and service. Remember that in his vision, Daniel saw the kings serving the King. Once again, Jesus set the example when He, the King of kings, took up a towel and bowl of a servant and washed His disciples' feet. At another time He told them, "For even the Son of Man did not come to be served, but to serve, and to give His life as a ransom for many" (Mark 10:45). We were not created to dominate each other, or to be dominated, but to serve one another equally as kings and priests in our Father's Kingdom. It is only when we understand our place and role in the Kingdom that we can fully appreciate the meaning of greatness.

PRINCIPLES

1. God's scepter—the defining characteristic of His rule—is justice.

2. We can live in victory and walk in confidence because the power of our enemy has been broken.

3. Jesus died on the cross and arose from the dead, not so much to take us to heaven as to bring us back into possession of the Kingdom we lost.

4. As children of God, we receive three specific things when we come into the Kingdom: *sovereignty, power,* and *greatness.*

5. Within the scope of our delegated sovereignty, we have absolute authority.

6. When we are restored to the Kingdom, we are restored to greatness, because we return to the place and environment for which we were created.

"The greatest discovery
is self-discovery."

THE PRIORITY OF THE KINGDOM

H ow important is the Kingdom of God? It is so important that our lives depend on it, literally. All that we are, all that we see and hear, the air we breathe, the food we eat, the water we drink—this physical world of ours issued forth from the Kingdom of God by His hand at creation. The Kingdom of God is at the center of everything. God's every action and activity is motivated by His desire and passion to see His Kingdom established on the earth.

How important to the Body of Christ is the message of the Kingdom of God? Frankly, we have nothing else to preach or teach. The message of the Kingdom is good news, and the Church exists to proclaim it. If we are doing our job, everything we are about will be Kingdom-focused: every sermon we preach, every Bible study we teach, every ministry we perform, every activity we accomplish, and every worship service we celebrate.

The Kingdom of God must be our highest priority; Jesus gave us no other commission. When He said, "Go and make disciples of all nations" (Matt. 28:19), He was commanding us to proclaim the Kingdom of God to a world that knew it not. Although the world is very familiar with the regimes of men, it is essentially ignorant of God's Kingdom. People of every nation need to know that God's Kingdom has come to earth, and that faith in Jesus Christ as Savior and Lord is the way in.

THE VISIBLE AND INVISIBLE WORLDS

We all live in two worlds: a visible, physical world that engages our five senses, and an invisible, spiritual world beyond what we see, feel, touch, smell, and hear in the natural. Many people dismiss the spiritual world as nothing more than superstition. Others acknowledge the existence of the spiritual, but believe it has little or no influence on their lives, or that it is a realm to be manipulated for their own benefit.

In truth, the spiritual world is more real than the natural one. First of all, the spiritual realm is larger than the physical realm, and, second, it is the realm from which the physical world originated. In other words, the invisible produced the visible. All things were created from the mind of a powerful Maker. What He imagined and planned in His mind He brought forth by the power of the Word.

For by Him all things were created, both in the heavens and on earth, visible and invisible, whether thrones or dominions or rulers or authorities—all things have been created through Him and for Him (Col. 1:16, NAS).

Therefore, the physical world reflects the spiritual world from which it came. Whatever we see in the physical world has a corresponding greater reality in the spiritual world. In his second letter to the church in Corinth, the apostle Paul addressed this duality of worlds in his effort to encourage his readers to look beyond their current temporary troubles to see the bigger picture beyond:

Therefore we do not lose heart. Though outwardly we are wasting away, yet inwardly we are being renewed day by day. For our light and momentary troubles are achieving for us an eternal glory that far outweighs them all. So we fix our eyes not on what is seen, but on what is unseen. For what is seen is temporary, but what is unseen is eternal (2 Cor. 4:16-18).

Because it is eternal, the invisible spiritual realm is more real than the visible physical realm, which is only temporary.

God's original purpose for creating the visible world was to establish His invisible Kingdom in that visible world—to manifest the spiritual in the physical. His plan for accomplishing this called for children who would inhabit visible physical bodies. For this reason He created man in His own image. He created them spirit, soul and body with the capacity to communicate with both realms, the realm of the spirit and the realm of the physical.

CREATED TO BE KINGS IN GOD'S WORLD

God created us as spirit "men," put us into physical bodies, some male and some female, placed us in a visible, physical world that He had created and said, "Dominate this for Me." In this way, God planned for us to rule and exercise control over the earth in His name. Through us, His rule of the heavenly Kingdom would be extended over the earth.

We were created as administrators of God's Kingdom on earth. It's that simple. Adam was the first, the prototype. Next came Eve, whom God fashioned from a part of Adam's side, and who ruled with Adam as a helper and equal partner. From them descended everyone who has ever lived or ever will live—an entire race of beings designed originally to dominate the physical realm so that the Kingdom dominion of God could cover the earth.

Adam and Eve disobeyed God and thereby forfeited their Kingdom rights. Satan, an interloper and outcast of Heaven, illegally usurped the throne that they abdicated, wreaking havoc ever since in the hearts and lives of people everywhere in every generation. He confuses our minds and blocks our ability to see God so that we neither know Him and what He is like, nor understand ourselves and who we are as children created in His likeness.

Because we are made in God's image, our hearts cry out for Him. But since our sin has separated us from Him and we cannot see Him, all we can do is reach out and fashion gods of our own making according to our own flawed understanding. Cut off from God, our source, we live lives characterized by fear, hopelessness, and despair. Worst of all, we live in fear of the One who created us to be like Him, who loves us with an undying love. We are all victims of Adam and Eve's disobedience. They hid from God out of fear, and we do the same, each in our own way. We inherited their sinful nature, becoming sons of disobedience as much as they.

A LITTLE HELP FROM HEAVEN

What could we do? In our fallen state we were helpless. Nothing that we might do in our own power would be sufficient to restore us to God's favor and to our former position. We needed help that only God could provide. That's why He sent Jesus Christ, His only begotten Son—

the second "Adam"—to undo the curse brought upon mankind by the first Adam. What the first Adam, the son of disobedience, lost, the second "Adam," the Son of obedience, restored. In a very real sense, this is like being raised from the dead: we who were spiritually dead in our sin have been brought to new life in Christ, the second Adam. Paul explained it to the Corinthians this way:

> But Christ has indeed been raised from the dead, the firstfruits of those who have fallen asleep. For since death came through a man, the resurrection of the dead comes also through a man. For as in Adam all die, so in Christ all will be made alive.... So it is written: "The first man Adam became a living being"; the last Adam, a life-giving spirit (1 Cor. 15:20-22,45).

Adam lost the Kingdom; Jesus restored the Kingdom. Adam did not lose heaven, because he was never in heaven; he was formed from the dust of the ground. Heaven was not Adam's home, and neither is it ours—ultimately. For believers, heaven is a waiting place until God's plan is fully consummated, but it is not our final destination. Heaven is a real place, the spiritual domain where God rules, but don't forget that He gave the earth to man as our domain to rule in His name: "The highest heavens belong to the Lord, but the earth he has given to man" (Ps. 115:16).

What the first Adam, the son of disobedience, lost, the second, "Adam," the Son of obedience, restored.

Ever since Adam's fall, God has been executing His plan to restore mankind to his place of dominion. Nothing takes God by surprise; nothing catches Him unprepared. God announced His plan for man's restoration in the same chapter of the Bible that describes man's fall. Speaking judgment on satan, that wily serpent who tricked mankind into sinning, God said, "I will put enmity between you and the woman, and between your offspring and hers; He will crush your head, and you will strike His heel" (Gen. 3:15).

Here the word *head* stands for authority. By their failure to stand up to satan and use their Kingdom authority to defeat him, Adam and Eve lost that authority. God promised, however, that the day would come when another would arise, an offspring and descendant of the woman, who would crush satan's authority, take back the power he stole, and restore the scepter of earth's domain to man, its rightful holder. That off-spring was Jesus Christ.

THE SON OF MAN AND THE ANCIENT OF DAYS

When Daniel interpreted Nebuchadnezzar's dream of the giant statue, he told the king that the kingdoms of men, represented by the statue, would be crushed and that the God of Heaven would establish in their place an eternal Kingdom under His rule. This Kingdom was represented in the dream by the rock not cut by human hands that shattered the great statue:

> *In the time of those kings, the God of heaven will set up a Kingdom that will never be destroyed, nor will it be left to another people. It will crush all those kingdoms and bring them to an end, but it will itself endure forever. This is the meaning of the vision of the rock cut out of a mountain, but not by human hands—a rock that broke the iron, the bronze, the clay, the silver and the gold to pieces* (Dan. 2:44-45a).

Furthermore, this eternal Kingdom would be established on the earth by a divine person whom Daniel referred to as a "son of man":

> *In my vision at night I looked, and there before me was one like a son of man, coming with the clouds of heaven. He approached the Ancient of Days and was led into His presence. He was given authority, glory and sovereign power; all peoples, nations and men of every language worshiped Him. His dominion is an everlasting dominion that will not pass away, and His kingdom is one that will never be destroyed* (Dan. 7:13-14).

This "son of man" came with the "clouds of heaven," which is a reference, not to literal clouds in the sky, but to hosts of angels. The son of man is led into the presence of the "Ancient of Days," another name for God the Father. Who is this "son of man"? For over 500 years, from the days of Daniel to the days of Jesus, the Jews regarded the term "son of man" as a reference to the Messiah, the Anointed One whom God would send to deliver His people. As the four Gospels in the New Testament make clear, Jesus adopted the term for Himself. "Son of Man" was Jesus' preferred self-designation.

It is no wonder that Jesus angered so many of the religious leaders of His day. They knew the prophecies of Daniel. When they heard Jesus call Himself the "Son of man," they understood that He was identifying Himself with the heavenly figure of Daniel 7:13-14, who appeared before the Ancient of Days to receive the "everlasting dominion." By so identifying Himself, Jesus was claiming to be the Messiah, the anointed Son of God.

We know Jesus as the Son of God, which He is. Why did He prefer the title "Son of man"? A passage in the fifth chapter of John's Gospel gives us a clue. It was the Sabbath, and Jesus had just healed a blind man at the pool of Siloam in Jerusalem. To the religious leaders, this constituted work, a violation of Sabbath law.

So, because Jesus was doing these things on the Sabbath, the Jews persecuted Him. Jesus said to them, "My Father is always at His work to this very day, and I, too, am working." For this reason the Jews tried all the harder to kill Him; not only was He breaking the Sabbath, but He was even calling God His own Father, making Himself equal with God. Jesus gave them this answer: "I tell you the truth, the Son can do nothing by Himself; He can do only what He sees His Father doing, because whatever the Father does the Son also does (John 5:16-19).

FATHER IS ALWAYS WORKING

The Jewish religious leaders took Jesus to task for working on the Sabbath. Jesus' reply was that He simply was following the example of His Father: "My Father is always at His work...and I, too, am working." What did Jesus mean by this statement? Doesn't the second chapter of Genesis tell us that God worked for six days in creation and then rested on the seventh? Wasn't that day of rest commemorated and established as a standard for God's people in the Sabbath law? Yet, Jesus said that the Father is *always* working. Maybe we have misunderstood the meaning of the Sabbath. Perhaps resting on the Sabbath means changing our *mode* of work, such as enjoying what we work for.

The important point here is that Jesus, as the Son of His Father, was committed to working whenever His Father worked, and doing whatever His Father was doing. Since the Father was always working, Jesus was always working, whether or not it was the Sabbath. Besides, Jesus plainly said, "The Sabbath was made for man, not man for the Sabbath. So the Son of Man is Lord even of the Sabbath" (Mark 2:27-28). God never intended for us to be slaves, bound to a strict legalistic interpretation of the day of "rest," but to live as free people in doing what is right and good at all times. By word and by example, Jesus showed us that it is *always* right to do good, even on the Sabbath.

As children of our Father, we also should be working whenever He is working. Jesus, as our elder brother, has set the example for us. The good work of the Kingdom of God never takes a holiday, and neither should we. Even when we are on vacation, and at other times when we are not at work at our jobs, we should still be working for the Kingdom. Too many times, when believers go on vacation they also take a break from the Lord and His church; they don't attend worship anywhere, they don't send in their tithe, they don't study God's Word, and they don't talk to anyone about the Lord and His Kingdom. This is not right. The work of the Kingdom never stops. Our Father is always working, and we should be working also.

A GIFT OF WATER

Once I was in the airport in Cincinnati, waiting for a flight. I walked into a snack shop to buy a bottle of water and the woman behind the counter recognized me. "You're the man on TV," she said. When I said, "Yes," she replied, "I'll get to you in a minute," and finished serving the two people ahead of me.

When my turn came, she asked, "What do you need?"

"Just a bottle of water."

"Anything else?" When I said no, she asked, "Can I buy you lunch? I run this shop. Anything you want, you can have, on the house."

So I ordered a sandwich and a bottle of juice. While she was serving these she began to open up. "I'm at the end of my rope," she confessed. "I'm almost at the point of committing suicide. When I woke up this morning I told God, 'If You don't give me a word today, I'm going to kill myself tonight.'" She told me she was hooked on heroin and trying to kick the habit. This woman was in terrible shape, extremely thin with sunken eyes. She said, "I'm so sick and tired of taking drugs. This is my nineteenth job. I asked God for a word today, and when I saw you, I knew He had answered my prayer."

All this time I was trying to listen politely, but was thinking, "I have a plane to catch. I don't have time for this." Then Jesus' words echoed in my mind, "My Father is always working, and I, too, am working." I knew I had to take time for this woman in need.

Then the strangest thing happened. This was a busy airport with people passing by constantly. I stood with that woman in that snack shop and ministered to her. We held hands over the counter, I prayed for her, took my lunch, gave her my card, and shared Christian references with her. During all that time, no one else came into that shop.

She noticed this and said, "No one else came in. That's impossible. God sent you to save my life."

No matter the time or the place or the circumstances, God is always working. He deliberately puts us in situations where we can minister to people. God is always working, and as His children, we must always be working also. That's what the Kingdom is all about.

SON OF GOD/SON OF MAN

Jesus shocked the religious leaders of His day when He spoke of God as His Father. At this time, the Jews generally had no concept or understanding of God as Father in a personal way. Therefore, Jesus' claim of such intimacy offended them. Fatherhood implies source. When we claim someone as father, we claim him as the source of who we are, suggesting we are made of the same "stuff." This is what Jesus was claiming when He called God His Father. The religious leaders understood His claim, which is why they persecuted Him. Jewish theology had no fatherhood image of God. They knew God was holy, just, and merciful, but they also saw Him as a terrifying judge, a consuming fire, a God to be feared. They did not know or see Him as a Father.

After His unprecedented claim to intimacy with God, Jesus went on to compare His activities and authority with those of His Father. Essentially, they were the same. Jesus exercised the same authority as His Father, particularly in matters of life and judgment:

For just as the Father raises the dead and gives them life, even so the Son gives life to whom He is pleased to give it. Moreover, the Father judges no one, but has entrusted all judgment to the Son...I tell you the truth, whoever hears My word and believes Him who sent Me has eternal life and will not be condemned; he has crossed over from death to life. I tell you the truth, a time is coming and has now come when the dead will hear the voice of the Son of God and those who hear will live. For as the Father has life in Himself, so He has granted the Son to have life in Himself. And He has given Him authority to judge because He is the Son of Man (John 5:21-22;24-27).

Jesus stated that He had the power to give life and the power to execute judgment over men, both of which were the purview of God alone. It is significant that Jesus refers to Himself as the "Son of God" in relation to His authority to give life, and as the "Son of Man" in relation to His authority to judge. Only God can give life, and since the Son of God is of the same essence—the same "stuff"—as the Father, the Son can also give life. On the other hand, the only one qualified or "legal" on earth to render judgment upon men is one who is an offspring of man. In order to qualify this offspring must be without sin, because only someone who has no sin of his own can bear the sins of others.

No one except Jesus has ever met this qualification, but He met it perfectly. Born of a woman, born of a virgin, born into the ancestral line of David, Jesus was a "son of man" because He was fully human. He was, as Paul said, the second "Adam." Unlike the first Adam, Jesus perfectly fulfilled God's original plan. Jesus did what Adam could not. Because He fulfilled His father's will perfectly and without sin, Jesus the Son of Man was qualified to judge the race of man. He passed that judgment at the cross where He took our sin guilt upon Himself, becoming sin for us (see 2 Cor. 5:21), and sentenced Himself to death. After judging our sin as the Son of Man, He was able, as the Son of God, to give us life.

Everything Jesus did in His earthly ministry—healing the sick, raising the dead, casting out demons, calming storms, feeding multitudes with mere handfuls of food—He did under His authority as the Son of Man. It was necessary for God to become a man in order to unleash His love and power in the earthly realms. By design, God gave

205

dominion of the earth to mankind, and only humans have "legal" jurisdiction here. That is why whenever God wants to do something in the earth He seeks to work through human agents. In Jesus He has the perfect man to initiate His work.

What does this mean to us? It means that even though Jesus was the Son of God, in the flesh He had no inherent advantages over us. Many of us tend to assume that because He was God in the flesh, Jesus was better equipped than we are. This is not so. Jesus had the same human stuff we do. He had a physical body that got tired and knew pain. He needed regular rest just as we do. He got hungry and needed food, and thirsty and needed drink. He faced the same temptations, yet never fell into sin. He operated under the power of the Holy Spirit and later gave that same Spirit to us. In everything He did He claimed His authority as the Son of Man. Because we have the same stuff, we have the same authority on earth. In Christ, we are authoritative on earth because we are human, just as He was.

A Kingdom of Ignorant Kings

The problem for so many of us is that we don't know who we are. We have become a kingdom of ignorant kings: ignorant of our identity, ability, power, and authority. Long ago we forgot, (if we ever knew), all that the enemy stole from us. Deposed, defeated, and dejected, like the prodigal son we sit in the mud and stench of the pigsty, nibbling on dry corn husks, never lifting the eyes of our spirit to behold the riches of our Father's estate that are ours if we will only reach out and claim them.

Our greatest enemy today is neither satan nor sin, because Jesus defeated both at the cross. Power is not the problem, either. We have power. That is why God did not send power to fix our problem. Our greatest enemy today is ignorance. What we don't know is killing us; or at least depriving us of a full and abundant life. The antidote for ignorance is knowledge, so God sent us His Word—His *living* Word in the person of His Son. Christ came to remove our ignorance about God and His Kingdom and to teach us of our heritage and kinship as children of the Father.

As long as we live in satan's darkness, we will never know that we are prisoners in our own territory, slaves of an illegal despot. We will never know we are the rightful rulers of this planet or that the devil is already a defeated enemy. Because we don't know any better, because we don't realize the power we have, we allow satan to run our lives, ravaging our bodies with sickness, draining our finances, destroying our marriages, messing up our kids with drugs and alcohol, and generally wreaking havoc.

Jesus is the light of the world. Light means knowledge. He came to show us who we really are and to expose the enemy's false kingdom. To put it another way, Jesus came to introduce us to ourselves and to call us to become the people God always knew we could be. He came to call us home.

Daniel 7:18 says that *"the saints of the Most High will receive the kingdom and will possess it forever—yes, for ever and ever."* A lot of believers are confused about the word *saint.* Some have been taught that saints are super-spiritual believers who lived high above the plane of everyone else and were awarded this exalted title after their deaths. In truth, *every* believer is a saint. When the Bible uses the word *saint,* it refers to *"every* child of God, *every* person who has entered the Kingdom through faith and trust in Christ as Savior and Lord." If you are a believer, you are a saint, and if you are a saint, you are an heir to the Kingdom of God.

The word *saint* comes from the same root as the word *sanctified.* To be *sanctified* means "to be set apart for a specific use; to be reserved for a special purpose." Think about your or your parents' wedding china. Is it set out for use on a common daily basis? Probably not. Fine china is usually reserved for very special occasions, such as major holidays when extended family members gather or when particularly honored guests are present. In this sense, the china is "sanctified" for use only on those occasions.

In the same way, we as saints are sanctified and set apart for God's special purpose. Collectively, we are the Church, the *ecclesia* in Greek, which also means the "called-out ones." We are the ones who will receive the Kingdom. We are the ones who will see our power, authority, and dominion restored. The Kingdom is not reserved for us alone, but for many, many others as well who are still outside and need to be brought in. That is why when Christ saved us and brought us into His Kingdom, He made us ambassadors so that we could go out and bring others in.

The Power to Change Our Life

Being saints also means that we are equipped and empowered to live in victory and exercise our dominion authority *right now*, in our everyday lives. We don't have to wait until we die or until Jesus returns to start enjoying our Kingdom benefits. That means we can take charge of our situation. It means we don't have to just scrape by from day to day barely making ends meet and desperately hanging on by our fingernails until the weekend or our next paycheck. We have Kingdom authority, and the Lord wants us to use it. He wants to bless us and bring us into the full potential He planted in us. He waits for us to avail ourselves in faith of all that He has made available to us. The choice is ours. It is a matter of grooming our Kingdom mentality, of learning to think, talk, and act like the royalty we are rather than like the galley slaves the devil has told us we are.

Unfortunately, this is not a natural mindset for us, and most believers have trouble making the change. So many look at their daily struggles with an attitude of despair or resignation, assuming that their circumstances will never improve, and they should simply try to make the best of it. They look at their mortgage or their water bill, then look at their empty wallet and ask, "How am I going to pay this?" Every day is filled with worry and stress over making ends meet. Is that any way for a king to think? What kind of a king complains or worries about paying his bills? It is all a matter of mentality.

Kingdom mentality says, "Bring on the problems. Let's have those challenges. I was born for this! This is just my kind of situation. Jesus and I are ready for anything. Come on; bring it on!" In a very real sense, Kingdom mentality is a warrior mentality. When necessary, kings go to war to defend their domain. They are willing to fight to the death in order to preserve their kingdom or to repel an attacker.

Kingship is all about protection, exercising authority, and reclaiming conquered territory. Sometimes it is even about taking the war right into the enemy's camp. The enemy is always lurking about somewhere, seeking to divide and conquer, to destroy our lives and to devour our substance. A slave mentality simply rolls over and yields to the enemy's demands, by assuming there is no other choice. Kingdom mentality faces the enemy square on and says, "No way! This is mine, and you are not going to rob me anymore! I am a king and a child of the King, and He has given this territory to me!" We must be willing to fight for what we know is ours. We must be ready to stand firm, take authority in Jesus' name, and reclaim what is ours by right.

PRIESTS WHO ARE ALSO KINGS

God is after building on earth a Kingdom of kings and priests; not two separate classes or castes, but two offices combined in the same person. Except for Jesus Christ, such a combination has not existed since Adam. A king is a royal executive, an administrator who exercises rule and judgment over a domain, while a priest is a spiritual representative between God and His people, and responsible for the spiritual well being of the nation. Adam needed neither a king nor a priest because he was already both. Before the fall, Adam was a king with administrative authority over the earthly domain, but was also a priest who enjoyed immediate, direct, and open fellowship with God.

God's original plan was for both king and priest to be the same person, but ever since the fall mankind has been trying to keep the two separate. When God delivered the nation of Israel from slavery in Egypt and called them to be His own people, He told them:

> *Now if you obey Me fully and keep My covenant, then out of all nations you will be My treasured possession. Although the whole earth is Mine, you will be for Me a kingdom of priests and a holy nation* (Exod. 19:5-6).

It was God's desire to bless all the nations and peoples of the earth through Israel, as He had promised Abraham centuries earlier. That is why He called the Israelites a "Kingdom of priests"; they were to be His representatives before the rest of the world. Although the nation of Israel as a whole failed in this regard, God did not abandon His original plan and design. In the fullness of time Jesus came, in the flesh a son of Israel, but in the Spirit, God's promised blessing to the world.

God has always wanted a priest with a crown. The problem with a democracy, republic, monarchy, dictatorship, or any other system of human government is that they separate the offices of king and priest. In a fallen world, it is probably a wise and necessary concession, because with sinful people the power of the state combined with the power of religion easily becomes overwhelmingly oppressive. Separate offices of king and priest can serve as balances against each other.

KING OF KINGS AND LORD OF LORDS

This separation is not what God originally designed or intended, and His purpose is to restore the offices of king and priest into one. Jesus fulfilled this when He came to earth. Like Adam, Jesus was (and is) a King. When Pilate asked Jesus, *"Are You the king of the Jews?"* (John 18:33), Jesus replied, *"My Kingdom is not of this world....My Kingdom is from another place....You are right in saying I am a king. In fact, for this reason I was born, and for this I came into the world, to testify to the truth"* (John 18:36-37a). He is the one the Book of Revelation calls *"King of kings and Lord of lords"* (Rev. 19:16).

At the same time, Jesus is also a priest. The New Testament Book of Hebrews presents Jesus as the great high priest who intercedes for us before the Father:

> *Therefore, since we have a great high priest who has gone through the heavens, Jesus the Son of God, let us hold firmly to the faith we profess. For we do not have a high priest who is unable to sympathize with our weaknesses, but we have one who has been tempted in every way, just as we are—yet was without sin. Let us then approach the throne of grace with confidence, so that we may receive mercy and find grace to help us in our time of need* (Heb. 4:14-16).

Jesus is the example, the prototype of what God desires for all His children. He wants us to be like Jesus, kings and priests in the world: kings to faithfully represent His government and execute His authority on the earth. He wants us to be priests who will represent His love, grace, and mercy to a world of people stumbling in the darkness with no knowledge either of Him or of His Kingdom. This is the purpose that lies behind His call to each of us when we came to Christ. As Peter wrote in his first New Testament letter:

But you are a chosen people, a royal priesthood, a holy nation, a people belonging to God, that you may declare the praises of Him who called you out of darkness into His wonderful light. Once you were not a people, but now you are the people of God; once you had not received mercy, but now you have received mercy (1 Pet. 2:9-10).

God's Super Agents in a Dark World

We, the Church, the "called-out ones" of Jesus Christ, are "a chosen people, a royal priesthood, a holy nation" called of God to "declare" His praises to a dark world. A royal priesthood is another way of saying that each one of us is both a king and a priest. Our Lord has called and commissioned each of us as His ambassadors—His agents—in leading those still trapped in darkness into the "wonderful light" of His Kingdom. Paul described our special calling this way:

Therefore, if anyone is in Christ, he is a new creation; the old has gone, the new has come! All this is from God, who reconciled us to Himself through Christ and gave us the ministry of reconciliation: that God was reconciling the world to Himself in Christ, not counting men's sins against them. And He has committed to us the message of reconciliation. We are therefore Christ's ambassadors, as though God were making His appeal through us. We implore you on Christ's behalf: Be reconciled to God. God made Him who had no sin to be sin for us, so that in Him we might become the righteousness of God (2 Cor. 5:17-21).

As followers of Christ, children of God, and citizens of His realm, we have no priority greater than proclaiming His Kingdom. Jesus devoted His earthly ministry to proclaiming the Kingdom, and His priority is ours as well. When Jesus came, He fulfilled the first part of His Father's plan of the ages: He restored the Kingdom of heaven on earth. Through His Spirit He has called each of us back home to our rightful place as royal citizens so that we can exercise our rights and authority right now and experience the victory of Kingdom living on a daily basis. He has also invited us to join Him in His work of reconciling the world to Himself. This is His focus and it must also be ours. Everything else is secondary. The Kingdom of God is all that matters, and apart from the Kingdom of God, nothing matters.

Jesus' command to us today is the same as that which He gave to His disciples 2,000 years ago: "As you go, preach this message: 'The kingdom of heaven is near'" (Matt. 10:7). We are His people, a royal priesthood, a holy nation, an army of ambassadors commissioned to bring reconciliation between God and the nations. Let us be careful to heed our Lord's command. *Let us preach the Kingdom of God!*

PRINCIPLES

1. The Kingdom of God must be our highest priority; Jesus gave us no other commission.

2. Whatever we see in the physical world has a corresponding greater reality in the spiritual world.

3. God sent Jesus Christ, His only begotten Son—the second "Adam"—to undo the curse brought upon mankind by the first Adam.

4. Our Father is always working, and we should be working also.

5. Only God can give life, and since the Son of God is of the same essence—the same "stuff"—as the Father, the Son can also give life.

6. Because He fulfilled His father's will perfectly and without sin, Jesus the Son of Man was qualified to judge the race of man.

7. In Christ, we are authoritative on earth because we are human, just as He was.

8. If you are a believer, you are a saint, and if you are a saint, you are an heir to the Kingdom of God.

9. Kingship is all about protection, exercising authority, and reclaiming conquered territory.

10. God's purpose is to restore the offices of king and priest into one.

11. The Kingdom of God is all that matters, and apart from the Kingdom of God, nothing matters.

"There is nothing as powerful as a
Concept, and nothing more dangerous
than a Misconception."

Chapter Nine

UNDERSTANDING THE KINGDOM CONCEPTS

The message of the Bible is about a King, a Kingdom, and His royal offspring. Every one of the 7 billion people on planet earth is seeking the Kingdom of God, which is their ultimate fulfillment. Every religion and activity of mankind is man's attempt to find the Kingdom. It is the pearl that out-values all pearls, and the only treasure that is worth all the other treasures of life. The Kingdom is life itself. Therefore it is imperative, crucial, and necessary that we all understand the concepts of kingdoms so that we can better appreciate the good news brought to earth by our Lord and Creator.

All true kingdoms contain the same characteristics and components. Here are concepts and principles of kingdoms that you should know and become familiar with. Study and apply them to the message of the Kingdom of God and heaven taught by the King Himself, Jesus Christ, in order to fully understand your purpose, potential, power, and position in life.

1. **The Kingdom Principle of Kings:** The king is the central component of a kingdom and embodies the essence of the kingdom. The king is the ultimate source of authority in the kingdom and through this authority establishes the kingdom. The sovereignty of the king is inherent in his royal authority. Here are some unique qualities about a king:

   • A king is never voted into power;

   • A king's authority is by birthright;

   • A king cannot be voted out of power;

   • A king's word is law in his territory;

- A king personally owns everything in his domain;
- A decree of the king is unchanging;
- The king chooses who will be a citizen of his kingdom;
- The king embodies the government of his kingdom;
- The presence of the king is the presence of his entire kingdom authority;
- The king measures his wealth by the wealth of his property;
- The home of the king expresses his nature; and,
- The name of the king is the essence of his power.

Therefore, the kingdom of heaven is like a king who wanted to settle accounts with his servants (Matt. 18:23).

Say to the Daughter of Zion, "See, your king comes to you, gentle and riding on a donkey, on a colt, the foal of a donkey" (Matt. 21:5).

The kingdom of heaven is like a king who prepared a wedding banquet for his son (Matt. 22:2).

"You are a king, then!" said Pilate. Jesus answered, "You are right in saying I am a king. In fact, for this reason I was born, and for this I came into the world, to testify to the truth. Everyone on the side of truth listens to Me" (John 18:37).

Now to the King eternal, immortal, invisible, the only God, be honor and glory for ever and ever. Amen (1 Tim. 1:17).

They will make war against the Lamb, but the Lamb will overcome them because He is Lord of lords and King of kings—and with Him will be His called, chosen and faithful followers (Rev. 17:14).

2. **The Kingdom Lordship Principle:** All true kings must have property or a domain over which they exercise rulership of dominion. Therefore, all true kings are personally legal owners of property, territory, or their domain. Another word for owner is "lord." All true kings are automatically lords. Kings own all

that is in their domain. Kings rule or command whatever is in their property or domain. Kings have absolute authority and control over their property. The king's wealth is measured by the wealth of his property. Kings can give their property to anyone they wish.

The earth is the Lord's, and everything in it, the world, and all who live in it; for He founded it upon the seas and established it upon the waters (Ps. 24:1-3).

How awesome is the Lord Most High, the great King over all the earth! (Ps. 47:2)

That if you confess with your mouth, "Jesus is Lord," and believe in your heart that God raised Him from the dead, you will be saved (Rom. 10:9-10).

...and every tongue confess that Jesus Christ is Lord, to the glory of God the Father (Phil. 2:11).

3. **The Kingdom Domain Principle:** The domain of a king is the territory over which he exercises authority, control, and dominion. The king owns his domain and can expand or extend it by the power of his might. The wealth of the domain determines the king's glory. When the king impacts the domain with his influence it is called his "kingdom" (king-dom-ain). The king can delegate authority to others to share in the governing and administration of his domain.

His dominion is an eternal dominion; His kingdom endures from generation to generation. All the peoples of the earth are regarded as nothing. He does as He pleases with the powers of heaven and the peoples of the earth. No one can hold back His hand or say to Him: "What have you done?" (Dan. 4:34-35)

4. **The Kingdom Constitution Principle:** The constitution of the kingdom is the documented will, intent, desires, and purposes of the king for his citizens and kingdom.

Since a king's word is supreme, who can say to him, "What are you doing?" Whoever obeys his command will come to no harm,

217

and the wise heart will know the proper time and procedure (Eccles. 8:4-5).

I delight in Your decrees; I will not neglect Your word (Ps. 119:16).

Your word, O Lord, is eternal; it stands firm in the heavens. Your faithfulness continues through all generations; You established the earth, and it endures. Your laws endure to this day, for all things serve You. If Your law had not been my delight, I would have perished in my affliction. I will never forget Your precepts, for by them You have preserved my life (Ps. 119:89-93).

Jesus answered, "It is written: 'Man does not live on bread alone, but on every word that comes from the mouth of God'" (Matt. 4:4).

5. **The Kingdom Law Principle:** The law of the kingdom is the proclaimed word, decrees, and edicts of the king, and these laws determine the standards and precepts by which the kingdom is to be governed.

And if we are careful to obey all this law before the Lord our God, as He has commanded us, that will be our righteousness (Deut. 6:25).

The law of the Lord is perfect, reviving the soul. The statutes of the Lord are trustworthy, making wise the simple. The precepts of the Lord are right, giving joy to the heart. The commands of the Lord are radiant, giving light to the eyes (Ps. 19:7-8).

The law from Your mouth is more precious to me than thousands of pieces of silver and gold (Ps. 119:72).

I tell you the truth, until heaven and earth disappear, not the smallest letter, not the least stroke of a pen, will by any means disappear from the Law until everything is accomplished (Matt. 5:18).

6. **The Kingdom Keys Principle:** The keys of the kingdom are the principles, precepts, laws, and systems by which the kingdom functions. The keys must be learned and applied by the citizens in order to appropriate the benefits and privileges of the kingdom.

I will give you the keys of the kingdom of heaven; whatever you bind on earth will be bound in heaven, and whatever you loose on earth will be loosed in heaven (Matt. 16:19).

7. **The Kingdom Citizenship Principle:** Citizenship in a kingdom is not a right but a privilege, and it is at the pleasure of the king himself. Citizens are chosen by the king and are beneficiaries of the king's pleasure and promises.

But our citizenship is in heaven. And we eagerly await a Savior from there, the Lord Jesus Christ, who, by the power that enables Him to bring everything under His control, will transform our lowly bodies so that they will be like His glorious body (Phil. 3:20-21).

Jesus said, "My kingdom is not of this world. If it were, My servants would fight to prevent My arrest by the Jews. But now My kingdom is from another place" (John 18:36).

But He continued, "You are from below; I am from above. You are of this world; I am not of this world (John 8:23).

They are not of the world, even as I am not of it (John 17:16).

8. **The Kingdom Royal Privilege Principle:** Royal privileges of the kingdom are the benefits the king affords his citizens. They serve as a security for being in good standing with the king.

But seek first His kingdom and His righteousness, and all these things will be given to you as well. Therefore do not worry about tomorrow (Matt. 6:33-34a).

And my God will meet all your needs according to His glorious riches in Christ Jesus (Phil. 4:19).

9. **The Kingdom Code of Ethics Principle:** This is the standard of conduct established by the king for the behavior and social relationships of his citizens. This is also the expectation of the king regarding the values and moral standards the citizens must adhere to. The code of ethics becomes the

foundation of the kingdom culture and manifests itself in the lifestyle of the citizens.

Do you not know that the wicked will not inherit the kingdom of God? Do not be deceived: Neither the sexually immoral nor idolaters nor adulterers nor male prostitutes nor homosexual offenders nor thieves nor the greedy nor drunkards nor slanderers nor swindlers will inherit the kingdom of God. And that is what some of you were. But you were washed, you were sanctified, you were justified in the name of the Lord Jesus Christ and by the Spirit of our God (1 Cor. 6:9-11).

10. **The Kingdom Commonwealth Principle:** All kingdoms function on the principle of a commonwealth. Commonwealth is the king's commitment to see that all of his citizens have equal access to the wealth and resources of the kingdom. This is important to the king because the quality of life of the citizens of a kingdom reflects the glory and reputation of the king. When the welfare of the king's citizens is excellent, then the king's reputation among other kings is honorable. Kingdoms provide for all the needs of their citizens; and the king is personally committed to and involved in the welfare of his citizens.

So do not worry, saying, "What shall we eat?" or "What shall we drink?" or "What shall we wear?" For the pagans run after all these things, and your heavenly Father knows that you need them. But seek first His kingdom and His righteousness, and all these things will be given to you as well (Matt. 6:31-33).

For the Lord God is a sun and shield; the Lord bestows favor and honor; no good thing does He withhold from those whose walk is blameless (Ps. 84:11).

11. **The Kingdom Culture Principle:** This is the lifestyle and way of life for the citizens manifested in their language, dress, eating habits, values, morals, and sense of self-worth and self-concept.

My prayer is not that You take them out of the world but that You protect them from the evil one. They are not of the world, even as I am not of it. Sanctify them by the truth; Your word is truth. As You sent Me into the world, I have sent them into the world. For them I sanctify Myself, that they too may be truly sanctified (John 17:15-19).

12. **The Kingdom Economy Principle:** All kingdoms operate on a system that secures and sustains the strength and viability of the kingdom. The system involves the kingdom government's providing opportunity for the citizens to participate in the benefits program of the kingdom's prosperity through contributing to the work ethic and culture of the kingdom. The kingdom economy usually involves a taxation system, investment opportunities, and creative development programs for the citizens.

Give, and it will be given to you. A good measure, pressed down, shaken together and running over, will be poured into your lap. For with the measure you use, it will be measured to you (Luke 6:38).

When Jesus heard this, He said to him, "You still lack one thing. Sell everything you have and give to the poor, and you will have treasure in heaven. Then come, follow Me" (Luke 18:22).

13. **The Kingdom Taxation Principle:** All kingdoms incorporate a taxation system, which allows its citizens to participate in the process of maintaining the kingdom infrastructure. The system allows the citizen to share in the kingdom's commonwealth and return a set portion of the king's resources back to the king. In essence, everything in a kingdom already belongs to the king, including the taxes required from the citizen, therefore taxation is simply the government's allowing its resources to pass through the hands of the citizen.

Tell us then, what is Your opinion? Is it right to pay taxes to Caesar or not? (Matt. 22:17)

Then He said to them, "Give to Caesar what is Caesar's, and to God what is God's" (Matt. 22:21b).

"In tithes and offerings. You are under a curse—the whole nation of you—because you are robbing Me. Bring the whole tithe into the storehouse, that there may be food in My house. Test Me in this," says the Lord Almighty, *"and see if I will not throw open the flood-gates of heaven and pour out so much blessing that you will not have room enough for it. I will prevent pests from devouring your crops, and the vines in your fields will not cast their fruit," says the Lord Almighty. "Then all the nations will call you blessed, for yours will be a delightful land," says the Lord Almighty* (Mal. 3:8b-12).

14. **The Kingdom Army Principle:** All kingdoms incorporate an army of security components to protect and defend their territory and citizens.

For He will command His angels concerning you to guard you in all your ways; they will lift you up in their hands, so that you will not strike your foot against a stone (Ps. 91:11-12).

15. **The Kingdom Delegated Authority Principle:** All kingdoms establish a representative system that delegates responsibility to appointed citizens to serve as envoys or ambassadors of the kingdom or state. Ambassadors personify and embody the king's authority and the kingdom or state. Ambassadors are the property and responsibility of the state and thus do not concern themselves with their own personal needs. Their primary purpose is to represent the interest of their kingdom.

As You sent Me into the world, I have sent them into the world. For them I sanctify Myself, that they too may be truly sanctified (John 17:18-19).

Again Jesus said, "Peace be with you! As the Father has sent Me, I am sending you." And with that He breathed on them and said, "Receive the Holy Spirit" (John 20:21-22).

16. **The Kingdom Ambassador Principle:** An ambassador speaks for the kingdom and does not represent himself, only his kingdom. The ambassador is the kingdom's agency for

conveying its will, desires, and purposes in the territory to which he or she is assigned.

And He has committed to us the message of reconciliation. We are therefore Christ's ambassadors, as though God were making His appeal through us (2 Cor. 5:19b-20).

17. **The Kingdom Education Principle:** All kingdoms establish a system and program for training and educating their citizens. The education system is designed to transfer, re-enforce, and inculcate the laws, values, morals, and manners of the king and the kingdom to succeeding generations and new citizens.

All this I have spoken while still with you. But the Counselor, the Holy Spirit, whom the Father will send in My name, will teach you all things and will remind you of everything I have said to you (John 14:25-26).

If you love Me, you will obey what I command. And I will ask the Father, and He will give you another Counselor to be with you forever—the Spirit of truth (John 14:15-17a).

18. **The Kingdom Administration Principle:** All kingdoms establish a system through which they administer their judgments and programs to the citizens. The administrative program is also designed to protect the right and privileges of the citizens and their access to the king's favor.

In the same way, let your light shine before men, that they may see your good deeds and praise your Father in heaven (Matt. 5:16).

19. **The Kingdom Principle of Glory:** The glory of the king is all and everything in the kingdom that represents and manifests the true nature of the king himself. The glory literally means "true essence or full weight."

Who among the gods is like You, O Lord? Who is like You—majestic in holiness, awesome in glory, working wonders? You stretched out Your right hand (Exod. 15:11-12a).

The heavens declare the glory of God; the skies proclaim the work of His hands (Ps. 19:1).

This is to My Father's glory, that you bear much fruit, showing yourselves to be My disciples (John 15:8).

20. **The Kingdom Principle of Worship:** The worship of a king is the expression of the citizen's gratitude and appreciation to the king for his favor, privileges, and security of being in his kingdom. Worship is also an indication of the perceived worth that the king is to the citizen. Worship always involves the offering of gifts to the king, indicating the citizen's awareness that all things that he enjoys are at the pleasure of the king and the acknowledgment that it all belongs to the king. Worship also expresses one's dependency on the king, which activates the king's obligation to care for citizens who proclaim his name as their king.

Worship the Lord your God, and His blessing will be on your food and water. I will take away sickness from among you, and none will miscarry or be barren in your land. I will give you a full life span (Exod. 23:25-26).

Do not worship any other god, for the Lord, whose name is Jealous, is a jealous God (Exod. 34:14).

Jesus said to him, "Away from Me, Satan! For it is written: 'Worship the Lord your God, and serve Him only'" (Matt. 4:10).

21. **The Kingdom Principle of Provision:** In all true kingdoms the king is obligated to provide for his citizens and thus he makes provisions at his own expense for their security and welfare.

I was young and now I am old, yet I have never seen the righteous forsaken or their children begging bread. They are always generous and lend freely; their children will be blessed (Ps. 37:25-26).

So do not worry, saying, "What shall we eat?" or "What shall we drink?" or "What shall we wear?" (Matt. 6:31).

22. **The Kingdom Principle of Influence:** All kingdoms are committed to making the influence of the king and his will felt throughout the entire kingdom.

He told them still another parable: "The kingdom of heaven is like yeast that a woman took and mixed into a large amount of flour until it worked all through the dough" (Matt. 13:33).

Therefore go and make disciples of all nations, baptizing them in the name of the Father and of the Son and of the Holy Spirit, and teaching them to obey everything I have commanded you. And surely I am with you always, to the very end of the age (Matt. 28:19-20).

23. **The Kingdom Principle of Royal Favor:** Royal favor is the sovereign prerogative of the king to extend a personal law to a citizen that positions that citizen to receive special privileges and advantages that are personally protected by the king.

And the Lord said, "I will cause all My goodness to pass in front of you, and I will proclaim My name, the Lord, in your presence. I will have mercy on whom I will have mercy, and I will have compassion on whom I will have compassion (Exod. 33:19).

24. **The Kingdom Principle of Decree:** A royal decree is a declaration of a king that becomes law to all. It is sustained by the king's personal commitment to bring the declaration or promise to pass.

Remember, O king, that according to the law of the Medes and Persians no decree or edict that the king issues can be changed (Dan. 6:15).

I tell you the truth, until heaven and earth disappear, not the smallest letter, not the least stroke of a pen, will by any means disappear from the Law until everything is accomplished (Matt. 5:18).

25. **The Kingdom Principle of Reputation:** The king's reputation is important to the king and is the source of the glory of his name. A king's reputation is created and sustained by the

conditions of his citizens and his kingdom. Therefore kings act in ways that are favorable to their name's sake.

For the sake of His great name the Lord will not reject His people, because the Lord was pleased to make you His own (1 Sam. 12:22).

For the sake of Your word and according to Your will, You have done this great thing and made it known to Your servant (2 Sam. 7:21).

26. **The Kingdom Principle of Giving to a King:** Giving to a king activates the king's obligation to demonstrate his glory and power to the giver and to prove that he is a greater king than all other kings. Giving to a king in his kingdom is the acknowledgment that all things belong to that king and the citizen is grateful. Because giving to a king is impossible (since all things already belong to the king), the act of giving benefits the citizen more than the king. Thus one should never come before a king empty-handed.

And she gave the king 120 talents of gold, large quantities of spices, and precious stones. Never again were so many spices brought in as those the queen of Sheba gave to King Solomon (1 Kings 10:10).

King Solomon was greater in riches and wisdom than all the other kings of the earth. The whole world sought audience with Solomon to hear the wisdom God had put in his heart. Year after year, everyone who came brought a gift—articles of silver and gold, robes, weapons and spices, and horses and mules (1 Kings 10:23-25).

From the above overview of kingdoms, one can see that a kingdom is more advantageous than a republic. Therefore it is more beneficial to be in a kingdom than a democracy or any other form of government.

I therefore challenge you to embrace and accept the invitation of the King, Jesus Christ, to come and renew your citizenship in the Kingdom of heaven by being born into the Kingdom of God through the reception of the Holy Spirit of the King, by accepting the provision of the redemptive work of the King Himself. This is your opportunity, not to join a religion or become a slave of rituals or traditions that have no practical meaning, but rather to migrate from the kingdom of darkness to the Kingdom of light and renew your heavenly immigration status on earth.

You were created to represent God and His heavenly government through your dominion over the territory of earth through the gift you possess. May you rediscover your true destiny through rediscovering your place in the Kingdom of God as His representative king-ruler over this colony called earth. You were born to be born-again. It is your choice and your destiny! Welcome home to your dominion, and acknowledge Him truly as King of the Kings and Lord of the lords.

Thy Kingdom come!

Bahamas Faith Ministries International

The Diplomat Center
Carmichael Road
P.O. Box N-9583
Nassau, Bahamas

TEL: (242) 341-6444
FAX (242) 361-2260

**Website:
http://www.bfmmm.com**

More Exciting Titles
by Dr. Myles Munroe

UNDERSTANDING YOUR POTENTIAL

This is a motivating, provocative look at the awesome potential trapped within you, waiting to be realized. This book will cause you to be uncomfortable with your present state of accomplishment and dissatisfied with resting on your past success.

ISBN 1-56043-046-X

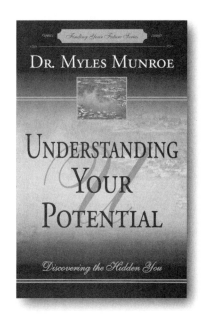

RELEASING YOUR POTENTIAL

Here is a complete, integrated, principles-centered approach to releasing the awesome potential trapped within you. If you are frustrated by your dreams, ideas, and visions, this book will show you a step-by-step pathway to releasing your potential and igniting the wheels of purpose and productivity.

ISBN 1-56043-072-9

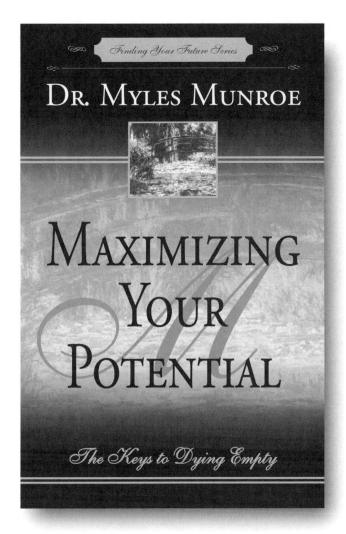

MAXIMIZING YOUR POTENTIAL

Are you bored with your latest success? Maybe you're frustrated at the prospect of retirement. This book will refire your passion for living! Learn to maximize the God-given potential lying dormant inside you through the practical, integrated, and penetrating concepts shared in this book. Go for the max—die empty!

ISBN 1-56043-105-9

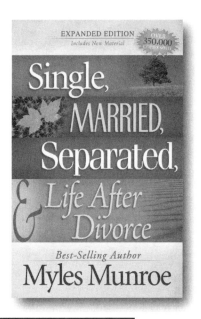

THE PURPOSE AND POWER OF PRAISE & WORSHIP

God's greatest desire and man's greatest need is for a Spirit to spirit relationship. God created an environment of His Presence in which man is to dwell and experience the fullness of this relationship. In this book, Dr. Munroe will help you discover this experience in your daily life. You are about to discover the awesome purpose and power of praise and worship.

ISBN 0-7684-2047-4

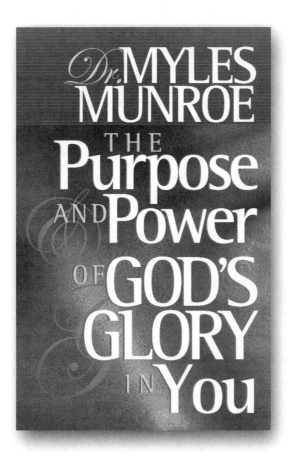

THE PURPOSE AND POWER OF GOD'S GLORY IN YOU

Everywhere we turn, we are surrounded by glory. There is glory in every tree and flower. There is the splendor in the rising and setting sun. Every living creature reflects its own glory. Man in his own way through his actions and character expresses an essence of glory. But the glory that we see in Creation is but the barest reflection of the greater glory of the Creator. Dr. Munroe surgically removes the religious rhetoric out of this most-oft used word, replacing it with words that will draw you into the powerful presence of the Lord. *The Purpose and Power of God's Glory In You* not only introduces you to the power of the glory but practically demonstrates how God longs to see His glory reflected through man.

ISBN 0-7684-2119-5

Available at your local Christian bookstore.

For more information and sample chapters,
visit www.destinyimage.com